STRONGER
TOGETHER

52 DEVOTIONS TO
STRENGTHEN KIDMIN LEADERS

BY BETH FRANK
AND OTHERS

Stronger Together: 52 Devotions to Strengthen Kidmin Leaders

© 2021 by Beth Frank. All rights reserved.

Published by KidzMatter
432 East Val Lane, Marion, IN 46952

Printed in the United States of America

Scripture taken from the NEW AMERICAN STANDARD BIBLE®, Copyright © 1960, 1962, 1963, 1968, 1971, 1972, 1973, 1975, 1977, 1995 by The Lockman Foundation. Used by permission.

ISBN 9781087973708 (Paperback)
ISBN 9781087973715 (ePub)

Stronger Together Logo by Beth Frank
Cover image © Shutter Stock / Arthimedes
Cover design and interior layout by Nicole Jones - kneecoalgrace@gmail.com
Edited by Amber Pike - amberpike.org

We dedicate this book
to you,
KIDMIN FRIENDS.
What you do
MATTERS!

A WORD FROM BETH FRANK

Dear Kidmin Friend,

It's easy to forget why you do what you do and to get lost in the week-to-week monotony of ministry. Hopefully this book will encourage you to step back and be reminded of what matters. You play a significant role in the kingdom.

We have asked several of our ministry friends to write to the kidmin community specifically to encourage you and speak life over your ministry and family. Don't forget, we are in this together - together with each other, and more importantly, together with Jesus. We are truly stronger together!

Colossians 3:24 tells us, "knowing that from the Lord you will receive the inheritance as your reward. You are serving the Lord Christ."

This book has 52 devotions, one for each week of the year. Read it before going into your week. Meditate on the scriptures in each chapter and open your heart to what the Holy Spirit has to say.

You are serving the Lord... even when it's tough.

You are serving the Lord... whether you have one kid in your class or one hundred.

You are serving the Lord... on the good days and the bad.

You are serving the Lord... even if it feels like what you do isn't making a difference.

What you do matters, friend. It's not babysitting. It's kidmin. And it's important.

Xo,

Beth

STRONGER TOGETHER

Beth Frank loves Jesus, her hubs, her three girls, and thinking creatively. Beth is the co-founder of KidzMatter. She also owns a design company called B Frank Design Co. She was inspired by her oldest daughter's autism diagnosis to write the book Ausomely Blessed.

The world, lately, hasn't felt very together. We are living in unprecedented times of loneliness, isolation, and division. It would seem that on most levels we are more divided than ever before. We've had the actual physical division of the quarantine required to stay safe from the Covid-19 pandemic during 2020. Every day, the news and social media posts show the ever-widening gap politically, socially, culturally, and even religiously. No, things definitely do not feel very together.

We, as Kidmin leaders and volunteers, minister to children and families that experience this division and loneliness as a brutal reality every single day. How can we effectively bring hope to their reality when we ourselves live facing the same challenges?

God did not intend for us to do life alone. We need each other and we need a team of people that we can do life with closely. As ministers of the gospel, we know this: it's one of the core pillars of our calling. I don't need to spend any time writing to kidmin people about the importance of community. We know it. It's what we are working toward week after week. We desire to bring people into community with God and each other. I would like to humbly interject a point here. Sometimes, during the mission to build community for the ones in our ministry, we lose it for ourselves.

Ministry life is hard and can be very isolating if we let it. Add to this the pressures and challenges of this current culture that we've already talked about, and we have the makings for a toxic stew. Right now, it is imperative that we not try to do ministry alone… that we not try to do life alone… that we not attempt to live out our calling without the help, support, and strength of others, and most importantly, Jesus. We need to be intentional about togetherness - togetherness with Jesus and togetherness with the people he's assigned for us to do life with. I need you, sweet ministry friend, and you need me.

How can we accomplish all this togetherness in the crazy, chaotic ministry lives that we live? It's not easy, but it is simple. We need to simply commit to making it happen. Simply be intentional. Simply schedule time for togetherness.

We need people. We need people that we have invested in and they have invested in us. We need people we have history with. You know those people, the ones that know the good, bad, and ugly about you. Maybe they even know you have a little crazy in you. Yeah, those people are the ones with whom we need to consciously and intentionally make the choice for togetherness. If you don't have people like that, start now developing and cultivating relationships where you can be real and vulnerable. Commit to building Hebrews 4:24-25 relationships: *"And let's consider how to encourage one another in love and good deeds, not abandoning our own meeting together, as is the habit of some people, but encouraging one another."*

This right here is what togetherness with the people closest to us should be all about. Am I thinking daily about how to influence those around me in love and good deeds? Am I continually thinking about how to be an encouragement to the people I am doing life with? It is so much easier to live together when the issues of life don't keep popping up. Issues will pop up, because we are human and live with humans. But if my focus is on how to encourage, build-up, and love others, I won't be focused on the issues. I won't be focused on how we think differently, or about division, if I am first focused on how I can encourage you in your own calling. I won't focus on the problem if I am first focused on loving the person.

Every week we tell the kids that we teach and the parents that we influence that they need a quiet time with God everyday. We ourselves can't forget about this. We need our time just sitting with our Savior and letting His truth flow in us while His love flows over us. We need this like the air we breath and the water we drink. It is impossible to do ministry without it. If we hope to have any type of togetherness horizontally in our relationships with people, it starts vertically with our relationship with our Father.

We need to check our Holy Spirit meter often. It shows when we try and do all that God has assigned for us in our own strength. All of the sudden, I realize I haven't been spending enough time, or enough quality time ,with Jesus. I am tired all the time and don't have the energy for the calling in front of me. Little things put me over the edge. I start dreaming about a life outside of ministry or a different life from the one God has placed me in. It becomes increasingly difficult for me to live in obedience to Scripture and respond biblically. I lose my hope in the future and my joy in the present.

These are all serious indicators that we have let the busyness of service inhibit us from what is most important and that's our togetherness with Jesus. If this is you, sweet friend, know that we all get here from time to time during our journey. There is no better day than today to commit to the togetherness with Jesus that you need. You will know the where, when, and how. Just schedule, be intentional, and make it happen.

The simple fact that you are holding this book tells me that you know the importance of what I just wrote and that you value and hold dear your relationship with your Creator. He is our hope and strength in this divided world. I pray the devotionals in this book will help you as you prioritize your time with Him and seek togetherness with God and the ones you serve. May you truly be stronger because we are in this together.

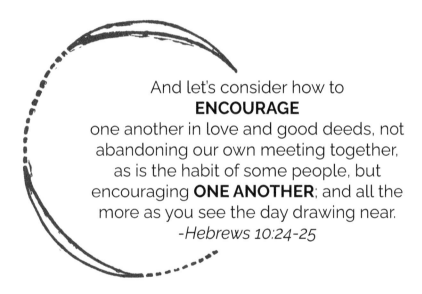

And let's consider how to
ENCOURAGE
one another in love and good deeds, not abandoning our own meeting together, as is the habit of some people, but encouraging **ONE ANOTHER**; and all the more as you see the day drawing near.
-Hebrews 10:24-25

Pray about it: *Schedule out some time today and commit to togetherness with God. Spend some time talking and listening to the Father. What is he saying to you?*

_____

_____

_____

_____

A FAMILY-FIRST MINDSET

***Ryan Frank** is a pastor, publisher, and entrepreneur. He serves as CEO of KidzMatter, co-founder of KidzMatter Mega-Con, and CEO of Frank Insurance Agency. Ryan and his wife, Beth, run several businesses and love to travel and spend time with their three daughters.*
ryanfrank.com

I've heard it a thousand times: Don't sacrifice your family on the altar of ministry. We've all seen ministry leaders do this very thing... they run nonstop. They go, go, go. They serve people. They build ministries only to look back one day and realize that they sacrificed their family in the process.

No one wants this.

People don't go into ministry hoping they'll lose their kids because of their ministry. People don't serve the Lord hoping they'll ruin their marriage because they give all they have to the church and leave little for their spouses.

The Bible gives some very stern warnings and reminders about keeping family first. 1 Timothy 5:8 says, *"But if anyone does not provide for his relatives, and especially for members of his household, he has denied the faith and is worse than an unbeliever."* Those are strong words, and they should cause us to pause and reflect on how we are doing at home.

Proverbs 11:29 says, *"Whoever troubles his own household will inherit the wind."* Think about that. What kind of inheritance is the wind? You can't even touch it. There is no real value to it. People who bring ruin on their family will only inherit wind.

None of us wants to ruin our family. None of us wants to become infidels in God's eyes because we have not taken care of our families.

I want you to have a family-first mindset!

More often than not, making more time for your family means compromising time somewhere else in life. Putting your family first means making sacrifices as necessary.

I learned this secret some years ago. Saying no doesn't have to mean never. It can mean "not right now."

In Proverbs 15:27 we are told, *"Whoever is greedy for unjust gain troubles his own household."* You and I must choose to make sacrifices for our family in an attempt to keep them first.

May the Lord
GIVE YOU INCREASE,
you and your children.
-Psalm 115:14

Do something about it: *Step back and evaluate.*
Do you have a family-first mindset?
Commit to spend some extra time with your family this week.

_____

_____

_____

FROM GENERATION TO GENERATION

__Amber Pike__ is the editor of KidzMatter Magazine, an author, a children's minister, and a momma whose passion is to see kids loving the Word of God and walking with Him!
www.amberpike.org

VBS during the summer I turned 16 was the year that God changed my life. This was my first year of teaching. I had a class of preschoolers and the theme for the week was becoming fishers of men.

Sitting at the snack tables one night, the director was asking the kids, "What are you going to do?"

"Go fish for Jesus!"

"What are you going to fish for?" "Fish!" sweet little voices answered.

Even though these little ones thought they were going to catch fish instead of people, seeing kids delight in God's Word changed me. It changed my future, actually. That was the day that God called me into the ministry. Very clearly, I felt God ask me to tell boys and girls about him for the rest of my life, to which I happily obeyed.

Kidmin leaders, what you do matters! You have been tasked with the all-important role of declaring his mighty acts to the next generation. It is not your role alone, you are partners with parents in this, but you are given this role.

You have been chosen. You have been called.

It is important, and it's rewarding. (I'm not sure there is anything more rewarding than watching a child accept Christ).

But the stakes are high; eternity is at stake. Satan doesn't want you to succeed. He doesn't want to see another child's eternity changed. So, he's going to throw hurdles in your way – difficult parents, budget cuts, hard-to-love kids, you name it. There will be days when you want to quit (and days when you can't imagine doing anything else).

Don't give up. When you feel overwhelmed and ministry gets hard, don't give up. Remember what is at stake! Remember why you were called. Remember that what you do matters!

I am blessed enough to actually have a picture of the day that God called me into the ministry. It's one of my most treasured possessions, actually. And every time I look back at those little faces, many of whoms names I have forgotten, I am reminded of something very important. And today, I want to remind you of this.

God has chosen you and called you to teach his children, to declare his mighty acts to the next generation. What you do matters.

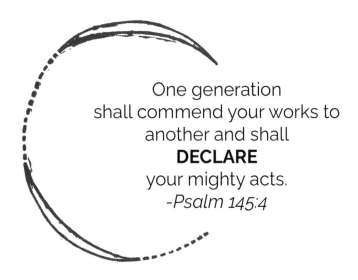

One generation
shall commend your works to
another and shall
DECLARE
your mighty acts.
-Psalm 145:4

Pray about it: *How do you feel about your calling? Has it become more of a chore or are you still excited to teach the next generation?*

_____

_____

_____

_____

_____

_____

_____

A MATTER OF 'FIRST IMPORTANCE'

***Joshua Cooley** is a longtime kid's ministry leader and a New York Times bestselling author whose many books include kids and youth devotionals www.joshuacooleyauthor.com*

Details, details, details.

As a kid's ministry leader, you know well the never-ending decisions, nuances, and moving parts that go into every week of your programs.

"Did we background check Bobby before he starts serving?"

"Did we find a sub for Sally, who's sick?"

"Did we ask Pastor Ned to announce the need for more nursery workers?"

"And good gravy! Who ordered the extra Goldfish, glitter glue, and graham crackers for this Sunday?!?!"

Phew! The sheer amount of details can be overwhelming.

It's also easy to let the newest fads or most recent technology distract us. We can quickly become sidetracked by a desire to "stay relevant," sacrificing truth for the latest methodology. When teaching Bible stories, it's not hard to slip into moralistic instruction instead of proclaiming the truth of God's Word. These are all easy traps to fall into.

1 Corinthians 15:3-4 provides a powerful tool for our battle. Here, the apostle Paul lifts our eyes from the mundane and the clamor to the glorious central truth of the gospel: the good news that Jesus died and rose again to redeem lost sinners. This passage refocuses our gaze and clarifies our mission.

These verses come near the end of Paul's long letter to the troubled Corinthian church, which was facing a litany of spiritual problems. Yet Paul seems to be taking the church by its collective shoulders, looking it dead in the eye, and saying, "Listen carefully. Above all, you've got to get this right. The gospel message is the deal-breaker." So it is with us.

The minutiae of kid's ministry is really important. Each Sunday can't function without your attention to the large and small details. So yes, find those subs, buy that glitter glue, and get Pastor Ned on board! But never minimize the matter of "first importance." Make the message of Jesus' death, burial, and resurrection central to everything you do as you serve kids and families. Believe it, pray it, cherish it, read it, memorize it, sing it, and proclaim it! Our Savior is worthy of all of it.

For I handed down to you as of
FIRST IMPORTANCE
what I also received, that Christ died for our sins
according to the Scriptures, and that
He was buried, and that He was
RAISED ON THE THIRD DAY
day according to the Scriptures.
-1 Corinthians 15:3-4

Think about it: Are there areas in which the gospel message is not a matter of first importance in your ministry?
What about in your personal life?

_____

_____

_____

_____

_____

_____

_____

_____

ETERNAL
AND INTIMATE

***Brittany Nelson** is the creator of Deeper KidMin (deeperkidmin.com), a digital hub of creative resources made FOR kidmin leaders BY kidmin leaders. Her other adventures include being a toddler mom, working part-time for her church in an administrative role, reading as many books as she can, volunteering with her husband's youth group, and drinking lots of herbal tea.*

One of the cool things about God is that His character is full of juxtapositions - opposite traits that shouldn't be able to co-exist in one person but do. He is a judge and yet merciful. He (in Jesus) is holy and yet human. And my favorite one is that He is eternal and yet intimate.

The same God who created the heavens and the earth – who built universes and exists outside of time – is the same God who wants a personal relationship with me.

It makes my heart sing when he pursues me in the midst of his busy schedule. He's got a lot going on, and yet he still makes time for me every day. He draws near to me just as I draw near to him, and even when he feels far away, he's not.

I'm reminded of the story of Elijah in 1 Kings 19:11-12. Elijah goes to stand out on the side of the mountain to wait for God to pass by...

> *"And a great and powerful wind was tearing out the mountains and breaking the rocks in pieces before the Lord; but the Lord was not in the wind. And after the wind there was an earthquake, but the Lord was not in the earthquake. And after the earthquake, a fire, but the Lord was not in the fire; and after the fire, a sound of a gentle blowing [whisper]".*

And do you know why Elijah could hear the gentle whisper of the Lord? Because God was near.

You can only hear the whispers of those right by your side. This story is a great reminder of God's power and his placement; of his grandeur and his grace.

Like with Elijah, God meets us where we are so he can lead us where he wants us to go. And he is faithful to be with us the whole time.

Too often, we think of God as a far-off being of great power. Which he is. But he's also a personal protector who is always nearby, whispering intimately to our hearts from his eternal glory.

"Go out and stand before me on the mountain," the Lord told him. And as Elijah stood there, **THE LORD PASSED BY**, and a mighty windstorm hit the mountain. It was such a terrible blast that the rocks were torn loose, but the Lord was not in the wind. After the wind there was an earthquake, but the Lord was not in the earthquake. And after the earthquake there was a fire, but the Lord was not in the fire. And after the fire there was the sound of a **GENTLE WHISPER**.
-1 Kings 19:11-12

Pray about it: Make time and space today to listen for the gentle whisper of the Lord, leaning into His intimate presence and eternal power.

_____
_____
_____
_____
_____
_____
_____

REAL TRUST

Jack Henry is a veteran family pastor and has served at various churches over the past 38 years. He is more compassionate now than ever and still longs to be used by God to produce Kingdom growth. You can reach him at oldkidspastor@gmail.com

When it comes to Gideon, readers actually have quite a bit to unpack in Judges 6:11 - Judges 8:32. Although this devotion can't dive into everything, l will highlight two major portions of Gideon's story. I highly suggest reading the entirety of the two chapters to get a full picture of Gideon and all God accomplished through him.

Gideon Tested God Using Fleece: You know the story. Read about it in Judges 6:36-40.

Gideon and the Army of 300: When God wanted Gideon to bring an army to take on the enormous Midianite army, Gideon brings 32,000 men as we see in Judges 7. This number is enough for Gideon to be comfortable with leading the charge. But you see, God has other plans. He decides to enlist a series of tests of His own on Gideon, reminiscent of the tests Gideon had for Him in the previous chapter.

Stop here and read Judges 7:1-8!

With just 300 men now, Gideon knows he has to rely on God to provide a miracle.

But God has an even odder plan in place. Go ahead and read Judges 7:15-22!

What Can We Learn from Gideon's Story?

God can work with a little bit of faith. Overall, we see that God can work through anyone, even timid believers of little faith. A leader isn't always the boldest and most extroverted. God often works through believers who come from the least of the least, like Gideon. Like me. When we're hiding from what scares us most, God compels us to tackle it head on.

God wants us to trust Him. Second, God doesn't allow metaphorical crutches. Although he plays along with Gideon's fleece tests, when it comes to the actual battle, he refuses to let Gideon have a cushion of a bulky army. Reducing him to the bare essentials of 300, they know they have to rely on God for a victory.

Like Gideon, we can often have various cushions that offer comfort. We can only hide on the threshing floor for so long before God pulls us out of our comfort zones to do his amazing work. If we have not learned this over this previous year, I wonder if we ever will? Trust God no matter what! You will be amazed at what He will do.

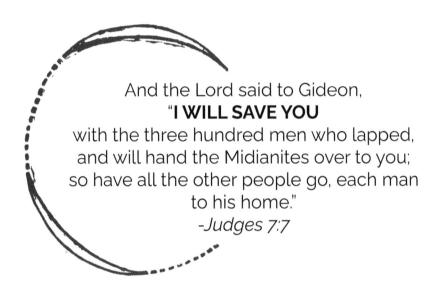

And the Lord said to Gideon,
"I WILL SAVE YOU
with the three hundred men who lapped,
and will hand the Midianites over to you;
so have all the other people go, each man
to his home."
-Judges 7:7

Pray about it: *What areas are you struggling to trust God in? Ask God to help you trust him more and allow him to move you out of your comfort zone.*

_____
_____
_____
_____
_____
_____
_____

EVERY RELATIONSHIP NEEDS THIS

***Beth Frank** loves Jesus, her hubs, her three girls, and thinking creatively. Beth is the co-founder of KidzMatter. She also owns a design company called B Frank Design Co. She was inspired by her oldest daughter's autism diagnosis to write the book Ausomely Blessed.*

Every year I choose a word for the year, something I feel God is laying on my heart that I need to focus on for the coming year. About five years ago the word I chose was "love". I began the year with lots of happy, romantic notions that this was going to be a wonderful year-long love fest. Because loving is easy, right? Wrong! Wow, little did I know what God had in store for me that year. The Lord taught me, and is still teaching me, all about biblical love and how I can love those that He has placed in my life. This has trickled down into my kids' lives and I am praying that they would be little love-bearers of Jesus to those around them. It isn't always easy for Momma and it isn't always easy for them, but here is a snapshot of some of the ways that Jesus is changing us in how we love those around us.

Biblical love means forgiveness. Listen, do not, and I repeat, do not pick love for your word of the year unless you pray yourself up and prepare yourself. I did not realize how much the enemy would come after me when I chose this word. Several things happened that year that were truly hard and forgiveness wasn't easy. But I am coming to the realization that I love Jesus more than being "right" or having justice served. I want a closeness with my Savior more than anything, and by forgiving as soon as possible, even when it is hard, I stay connected with Him.

Love prefers others. My girls and I talk about preferring others lots lately. Last night Londyn was complaining about having a certain child in her VBS group. He really didn't seem to understand everything that was going on and he needed lots of extra help during the evening which slowed her group down. This was a perfect love teachable moment. We explained to Londyn that this was a great opportunity for her. She had a chance to share the love of Jesus with someone who really needed it! We wanted her to see this as a special assignment that she had been given to reach out to a little boy that needed lots of love. God placed them in a group together for a reason and Londyn needed to be sensitive to God's leading.

My heart for my girls is that they would lead in love, but then I become so convicted after conversations like this because I begin to ask myself those same questions. Do I love those that are uneasy to love? Am I sensitive to God's leading and recognizing the special love assignments he has given to me? What is my frustration level with those in my life that seem to need extra care and extra consideration? Ouch! God is teaching me through my girls, and in lots of other situations, to put others and their needs ahead of my wants, wishes, and desires.

If I speak with the tongues of mankind and of angels, but do not have love, I have become a noisy gong or a clanging cymbal. If I have the gift of prophecy and know all mysteries and all knowledge, and if I have all faith so as to remove mountains, but do not have love, I am nothing. And if I give away all my possessions to charity, and if I surrender my body so that I may glory, but do not have love, it does me no good. Love is patient, love is kind, it is not jealous; love does not brag, it is not arrogant. It does not act disgracefully, it does not seek its own benefit; it is not provoked, does not keep an account of a wrong suffered, it does not rejoice in unrighteousness, but rejoices with the truth; it keeps every confidence, it believes all things, hopes all things, endures all things.

LOVE NEVER FAILS

-1 Corinthians 13:1-8a

Pray about it: *I challenge you to look at your world through the lens of biblical love. Are the key relationships in your life thriving through I Corinthians 13 love? Are you pursing relationships with hard to love people? When you make loving others a priority, God will stretch you in ways you never imagined, but the blessings are so worth it!*

_____

_____

_____

RISE UP!

***Corinne Noble** is a children's pastor, curriculum creator, and author. She enjoys writing curriculum, creating set designs, and sharing her ideas with other kidmin leaders at kmccurriculum.com.*

Do you find yourself feeling like you will never have enough time to get everything done? Well, you are definitely not alone there. I have felt that way many times, but recently have found a way to make much-needed room and time for getting things accomplished. Are you ready to hear what it is? I started waking up at 5 am most weekday mornings. I know I may have lost some of you there, but believe me, I wasn't always a morning person. It's still hard some days to drag myself out of bed, but the days I choose to rise up early are always my best days.

Don't take my word for it! The Bible has something to say about the benefits of rising up early and spending time with God in the morning. Psalm 5:3 says, "In the morning, Lord, You will hear my voice; In the morning I will present my prayer to You and be on the watch." David knew the morning was a great time to spend time in prayer with God. He also mentions rising "before dawn" to cry out and wait on the Lord in Psalm 119:147.

We can turn to the New Testament and learn from the best example, Jesus. Mark 1:35 says, *"And in the early morning, while it was still dark, Jesus got up, left the house, and went away to a secluded place, and prayed there for a time."* I used to say that if the sun was down, it means that we aren't supposed to be up, but this verse changed my mind. Jesus knew the benefit of rising up before the sun to spend alone time with God.

Let me tell you about a few of the things I love about rising up early and the benefits I have seen from this practice in my life.

1. I make time to give God the first fruits of my time and day. Before I look at my phone, begin working, or even eat breakfast, I take the time to read my Bible and pray. On the days I choose not to wake up early, I often fail to make this a priority.

2. I have the opportunity to watch the sun rise. I love sitting in my backyard, when the weather is warm enough, with a cup of coffee and my Bible watching the sun rise. It is so peaceful and unlike anything else.

3. I begin my days productively. I have a little boy named Peter who is about one and a half years old who needs my attention most hours of the day. When I choose to rise up early, I am able to begin my work while everyone else in the house is still sleeping. The silence is truly golden and hard to find these days. If I can even get in 1-2 hours of work in the morning, I feel so much more productive and less stressed for the rest of the day.

Give the practice of rising up early a try, even if you would not consider yourself a morning person.

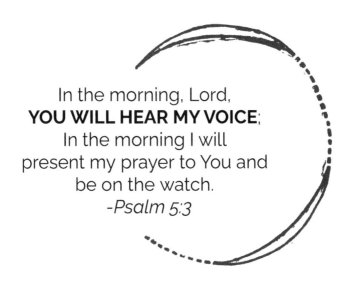

In the morning, Lord,
YOU WILL HEAR MY VOICE;
In the morning I will
present my prayer to You and
be on the watch.
-Psalm 5:3

Do something about it: Take a look at when you normally wake up and try getting up a half hour or an hour earlier to start. After a week or so, try waking up even earlier. Does rising up early make a difference in your soul, stress-level, and schedule?

_____

_____

_____

_____

HOW'S YOUR MEMORY?

Corey Jones is the Executive Pastor at Southern Hills, the Church at City Station and in his free time he helps leaders take their next steps to grow a healthy church.
www.CoreyRayJones.com

When my wife asked me about getting a new car, it caught me off guard. You see, just a few years earlier we were blessed with a great deal, and in my eyes, I still saw a car with few miles and only a couple of scratches and dents. When my wife saw the car, she saw the stuttering transmission and knew it would be just a matter of time before we would be calling a tow truck. This is when it hit me, remembering the blessings of God changes your perspective.

As we drove down the road talking about remembering the blessings of God, we remembered friends who were thrilled with God answering their prayers for a job, and then just a few months later, complaining about the stresses of work. We thought about fathers who had prayed and prayed to become a dad and now are at a place of exasperating their children. And we thought about how we have become so quick to complain instead of remembering the faithfulness of our Lord.

We see in scripture where God's people are praising God for the manna one minute and then as their memory quickly fades, they begin complaining about only having manna to eat. The Israelites memory fades away from the things of God.

We see Elijah at Mount Carmel where God answers his prayer by sending down fire to burn up the sacrifice and then a few verses later Elijah was afraid of Jezebel and ran for his life. Elijah failed to remember.

But think of the boy David. When all of Israel saw a Philistine giant, David said, *"The Lord who saved me from the paw of the lion and the paw of the bear, He will save me from the hand of this Philistine"* (1 Samuel 17:37). David remembered the deeds of the Lord and this changed his entire perspective.

In this world, you will have trouble. Your car transmission might be slipping, your job might be causing you stress, or maybe right after calling down fire from Heaven a queen calls for your execution. No matter what trouble comes your way, fix your eyes of the Lord and remember His faithfulness.

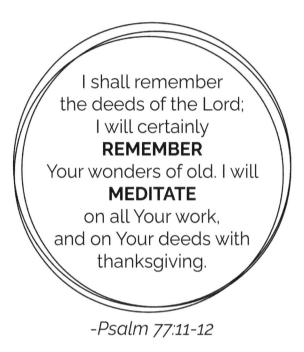

I shall remember
the deeds of the Lord;
I will certainly
REMEMBER
Your wonders of old. I will
MEDITATE
on all Your work,
and on Your deeds with
thanksgiving.

-Psalm 77:11-12

Think about it: *Have my thoughts today revolved around my problems or my Lord?*

_____

_____

_____

ENERGIZED TO SERVE HIM

Vanessa Myers is a children's minister, author, and blogger who loves to create resources for families to help them grow in their faith together. www.vanessamyers.org

I am a morning person. I am probably that person that all you non-morning people hate. How can you get up so early? Why are you talking? Why are you so happy? Why are you singing? Please stop! Nobody likes a happy morning person.

My husband and I are total opposites. He's that non-morning person. He really hates waking up. For the past eighteen years, we have learned to be respectful of each other in the mornings. That means don't talk. I smile at him and tell him good-bye, but that's about it. I don't know why I am so happy in the mornings. I just am. I love the early mornings because they are so peaceful. I love having my quiet time with the Lord. I get excited to see what God has in store for me each day.

People often ask me, "How do you have the energy to do all that you do?" My mother says that God gave me the gift of energy. And I believe it! I somehow can wake up ready to go and just keep going. Only God can provide me with the energy to do all I need to do.

I have a water bottle that a family at church gave me one year for Christmas. On it is a quote from Charles Stanley: "The awareness of God's presence energizes us for our work." Are you aware of God every morning when you wake up? Try something for me this week...before your feet even hit the floor, go to God in prayer. Give Him praise. Thank Him for another day. Thank Him you are alive. Then, be still (but don't fall asleep). Be aware of His presence as you sit in silence. This should make you feel ready and energized for the day and ready to do His work.

I know it's hard to be excited in the morning. I get it. But try to start your day with the Lord. I promise this will help you. Tell God you are ready to serve Him and ask Him to help you see Him in every part of the day.

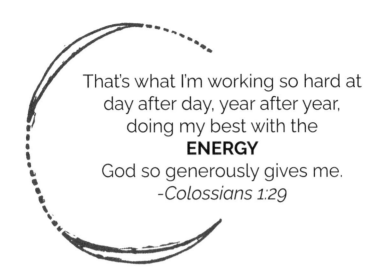

That's what I'm working so hard at
day after day, year after year,
doing my best with the
ENERGY
God so generously gives me.
-Colossians 1:29

Do something about it: *Start each day this week in prayer. Before your feet hit the floor and before you grab your phone, pray.*
Does it energize you for the day?

_____

_____

_____

_____

_____

_____

_____

_____

DOING VS. PLANNING

Amy Bates is a long-time children's director, and excited about learning new things. She is loving the second phase of her life with her husband and grown children, whom she loves to spend time with when they can organize their busy schedules together!

I would never plan a trip without doing my research—reading up on places to stay, what to do and where to eat, and talking to people who have been before me. I would diligently plan to ensure a successful trip.

A mentor once said something that made perfect sense. As we were digging deep into what matters most to me professionally, I realized that I spent the majority of my life DOING my "job" and not enough time IN my "job". Meaning—most of my time was spent doing daily tasks to keep going. To stay ahead. To not miss deadlines. To help others when asked. To get the work done. To always be ready. And the list goes on!

I hadn't taken much time to sit back and dream big. To invest undistracted time to set big goals. To work on long-range plans. To get out of my work surroundings and experience God. To fill a blank wall with ideas on Post-it Notes. To gather an eclectic group of people and ask questions. To listen to what others were saying.

It makes sense. If you want to grow and become better, you need to spend part of your time dreaming, goal-setting and listening. Working on projects that may not fit exactly into your day-to-day plans is key to your success. It ultimately supports the WHY you do what you do. You can't achieve success without drawing a roadmap of where you want to go and how to get there.

It's not always easy—Sunday's lesson isn't complete, volunteers are canceling, copies need to be made, the youth pastor needs your help, or the senior pastor has added another task to your list. If we don't have a well-defined roadmap of where we are headed, we will never get to where we want to be. Sure, our programs will continue, but will they remain relevant?

The key is to build time IN your ministry into your schedule. It's not easy,

I know. Reorganizing your schedule to accommodate this switch from DOING ministry to being IN ministry is hard. It takes real effort to not get caught up in distractions, and to stay focused on dreaming, reading, planning and connecting with others. Just like planning a vacation, we need to invest in what's further down the road... not just what's around the corner. There's an advantage to taking the time to focus on where you want to be!

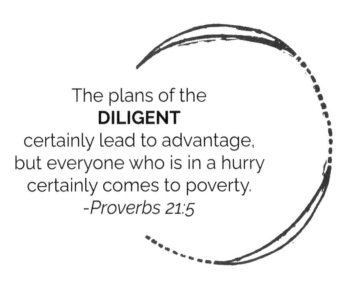

The plans of the
DILIGENT
certainly lead to advantage,
but everyone who is in a hurry
certainly comes to poverty.
-Proverbs 21:5

Think about it: How can you build some dreaming time into your schedule? Are you prepared for those dreams to come true?

_____

_____

_____

_____

CREATIVE KIDMIN

Josh Zello is husband to Hannah, father to Avery, and preschool pastor at nineteen:ten church in Boerne, TX. He's passionate about preschoolers, gospel-centered ministry, and crazy socks.
www.preschoolpastor.com

Think about it: the "before."

I mean, before God spoke. There was nothing. None of us can fully comprehend what this vast nothingness was like. Then God spoke up, and everything changed. By his Word, God created everything you can see and everything you can't see. The birds in the air, spoken into existence by the Creator. The rocks in your yard, created by the Rock of Ages. The children you minister to each and every week, knit together in the wombs of their mothers.

How amazing this truth is!

And how amazing that God created us in his image, also as creators.

Yes, we can't speak things into existence out of nothing, but we're called to cultivate and create like our Heavenly Father.

If you've been placed and called in a kids' ministry, you're called to cultivate and create within that ministry. Don't sit back and say "But not me, I'm not creative!" You have been created by the most creative One of them in all of eternity, and he made us to reflect Him.

Part of your role as a minister is creator. You get to create teams that reflect God's fellowship and unity. You get to create lessons that reflect God's knowledge and wisdom. You get to create vision that reflects God's insight and leadership. You get to cultivate the hearts of the children you serve in a way that reflects the perfect love of the Father.

Next time you're out and about, look around, and take in the creation of the Creator. Notice how each and everything that God made reflects some part of Him. Kidmin Leader, this is your best way to get inspiration! Spend time in creation, and then get to work creating alongside the

Creator, to reflect Him to the world you're called to serve.

It's okay to start small. Maybe you start out with a created prop for Sunday's lesson. Maybe you sit down and think about your kidmin vision, if you haven't already created that. Maybe you look at next month's theme, and begin brainstorming what needs to be created to show kids Jesus. Maybe you can create a team to pray for each child in your ministry by name.

Whatever your capacity, go ahead and get started! Create and reflect the Creator God.

In the beginning God
CREATED
the heavens and the earth."
-Genesis 1:1

Do something about it: *Do you consider yourself creative? Why or why not? What's one step that you can take today to begin to create and cultivate in your kids' ministry? Who can you ask to come alongside you as you begin to challenge yourself to be more creative for the glory of Jesus?*

_____

_____

_____

DISCIPLINE:
DO I HAVE WHAT IT TAKES?

Tashena Anderson-Place is the New Life Kids Coordinator/Worship Leader for New Life Kids at Trinity New Life Church in Odessa, FL. Tashena is a God fearing, wife, mom, and friend, a lover of Jesus that is honored to develop the next generation of disciples.

When we face challenges in life or feel pushed to try something new, we immediately get either nervous or excited, doubtful even. It is like we go through stages of talking ourselves in and out of the situation.

Does this sound familiar?

- "I can do anything I set my mind too!"
- "I'd be great at that… maybe."
- "I was born to do this!"
- "I'm too old, they won't consider me. It's a lot of work."

This is exactly what keeps us in limbo, unable to take the leap, unable to discern the voice of God. I call this being dazed and confused. It is a tactic used in spiritual warfare.

Here is an example. When you are faced with a challenging situation like getting your child to the car but the biggest bug you've ever seen is blocking the way, you have to think of a plan! There is no way you or your child will make it through without it seeing the both of you. So, as a parent you do what you believe is best, the dazed and confused tactic! You spray the bug with just enough bug spray to make it weak and vulnerable. It is no longer a THREAT to you both. It is fumbling all around and now you can take advantage of the situation. Off to the car you go!

This is exactly what the enemy does to us. When we are on the journey of life, the enemy sees us as a threat. He wants to get past us by all means necessary - through our thoughts, through those around us, and through our beliefs. He will keep spraying us with doubt, hurt, and pain so that we are vulnerable and not focused on our true purpose, the gift living inside of us. He is afraid that you will notice who you truly are and who your true Father is.

In these situations, we need to realize that we are chosen. God loved us so much and wanted to dwell with us forever that He sent his only son Jesus to the cross for US. Not for any special reason, but just because he loves us. Do not let the enemy poke holes in the armor that God has given you. Put on God's vision so that you can see through his eyes. You are everything that God says you are!

- His child
- Made in His image
- Filled with His spirit
- A mighty warrior

If this were not true, do you think the devil would spend as much time on us? No, he wouldn't, but since he can see us in glory, we threaten his agenda.

Everything you need to accomplish God's will is already inside of you. He will continue to build you up in the anointing, in the calling that he has placed on your life. You are going to feel weary, stay focused, and lean in even closer on those days. Just know you have what it takes because GOD says so! You have what it takes, you just have to activate it!

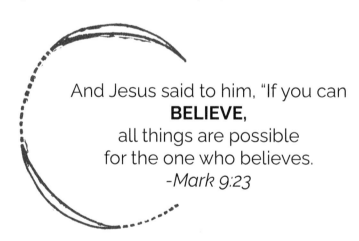

And Jesus said to him, "If you can **BELIEVE,** all things are possible for the one who believes. -*Mark 9:23*

Do something about it: Repeat the following... I am who he says I am. I believe in me. I will not give up! I will turn my eyes to Jesus and let him lead.

_____

_____

UNDILUTED TRUTH

Arlene Pellicane *is a speaker, host of the Happy Home podcast, and author of several books including Parents Rising and Screen Kids. You can meet her family in the documentary Screen Kids: In Their Own Words.*
www.ArlenePellicane.com
www.HappyHomeUniversity.com/film

My husband James is a diluter.

He dilutes fruit juice with water. He dilutes hand soap to make it last longer. He adds water to the shampoo bottle. And friends, he even dilutes my family's maple syrup.

When we're gathered around the breakfast table with hot, yummy pancakes, we all know one thing. Our maple syrup will be watery and thin. It will need to be applied quite generously to have any taste at all.

One glorious day, the maple syrup *finally* ran out. When I bought new maple syrup from the store, I roared to my husband, "You will not touch this syrup!"

Maple syrup is meant to be enjoyed undiluted.

This is how the Word of God should be consumed - undiluted. We should not water down the Scriptures.

You might say King Jeroboam in the Old Testament was a diluter.

In 1 Kings 13, we learn that a man of God issues a warning to King Jeroboam. He says that one day his son Josiah will sacrifice the priests of the high places on the altar. He will clean up house and get rid of those who practice idolatry. Jeroboam didn't repent upon these words. Instead, he tried to seize the man of God, but God withered his hand. He asked the man of God to pray for him and his hand was restored.

You would think after such a dramatic episode that King Jeroboam would heed the words of the man of God. But no, he didn't repent and instead appointed more priests for the high places. He disobeyed God's strict requirements for the priesthood. *Anyone* who wanted to become a priest could be one. Talk about a watered-down priesthood!

This sin did not go unpunished. The Bible says it led to the downfall and obliteration of Jeroboam's house.

Friend, if you choose to dilute your juice or even your maple syrup, it will not cause major problems in your life. But if you dilute the Word of God, trouble will follow. For King Jeroboam, it cost him the legacy of his family.

It says in Psalm 119:102-103, *"I have not turned aside from Your judgments, for You Yourself have taught me. How sweet are Your words to my taste! Yes, sweeter than honey to my mouth!"*

Sweet like undiluted maple syrup!

Since my declaration of "You will not touch this syrup!" my family has been enjoying maple syrup as it was designed to be eaten. Let us rise up, and more importantly, declare in our ministry, "We will not alter the Word of God or water it down to make the message more palatable." The undiluted Word of God is powerful and active, making life truly sweet and worth living.

After this event, Jeroboam did not abandon his evil way, but he again appointed priests of the high places from all the people, anyone who wanted, he ordained, and he became one of the priests of the high places.
-1 Kings 13: 33

Pray about it: Ask the Lord to reveal the answer to this question: Lord, am I diluting Your Word in any way? What can I do to make sure our ministry aligns with the Bible and not popular culture?

_____

_____

_____

THE GIFT OF ENCOURAGEMENT

Ryan Frank is a pastor, publisher, and entrepreneur. He serves as CEO of KidzMatter, co-founder of KidzMatter Mega-Con, and CEO of Frank Insurance Agency. Ryan and his wife, Beth, run several businesses and love to travel and spend time with their three daughters.
ryanfrank.com

There have been a handful of times in my life when I have been given an award or a plaque. I have been given these more so in my adult life. As a kid, I was never good at sports. I was a C-D student, and I wasn't athletic. Honor roll, athletic awards, and ribbons - they never really came my way.

Since I have received only a handful of awards in my life, it makes them special. I in no way want to say that those aren't important to me, because they are. However, I have learned that there is something that is worth so much more than an award, and worth so much more than a trophy. It's worth more than a cash prize or a gift. It is a word of encouragement.

Aren't words of encouragement great? I mean, they are awesome. I am actually writing this right outside of Starbucks. I'm at Starbucks because someone sent me a $10 gift card by email just to encourage me.

As I was using that gift card, I thought, you know what? Encouragement is so powerful. Encouragement... just an encouraging word, a thank you for being there, or an "I appreciate you." Maybe a "This ministry is better because of you," "These kids are better because of you," "These families are better because of you." Even tangibly, just saying, "Thank you for arriving early," "Thank you for sticking around late," "Thanks for putting in the extra mile and delivering that report," "Thank you for picking her up and bringing her over here," or "It's been a while since I have said thank you, but let me say thank you."

Those words of encouragement are fuel to people. They mean the world. Here's the thing, though. They are grossly, grossly underpriced. They are so cheap. It doesn't cost you anything to express thanks. It costs you nothing to look someone in the eye and say thank you. It costs you nothing to send somebody a text message and say thank you, but it is so appreciated.

Think of someone that you can encourage today. Then tomorrow, I want you to think of someone else that you can encourage. Then the next day, and on and on, keep encouraging.

I want you to live in a lifestyle of gratitude. Sometimes people ask me, "Ryan, you're always telling people thanks. Why are you so grateful?" Part of the reason I'm so grateful is because I put systems in my life that will help me be grateful. One of those systems I've used for about the last 15 years, is I have sent a thank you card to somebody every day of my life. Every day of my life, I send somebody a text and say thank you. Every day of my life, I try to find at least one person to look them in the eye and to just make their day, to compliment them, and to encourage them.

Those systems in my life help shape my mindset; they make me an appreciative person. I want you to be your team's biggest cheerleader. Your volunteers, your employees, your staff, and your family, I want you to cheerlead them like nobody else because encouragement goes a long way. Are you ready to do it?

Choose to encourage somebody today. Then choose to encourage somebody else, then choose to encourage somebody else, and then choose to encourage somebody else. When you become an encourager, your relational equity with people skyrockets. People love it. People will gravitate towards you. They'll be ready to help you with whatever you need. They'll be there for you, and they'll have a deep appreciation for you because you are appreciating them.

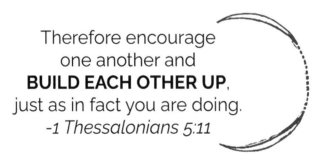

Therefore encourage
one another and
BUILD EACH OTHER UP,
just as in fact you are doing.
-1 Thessalonians 5:11

Pray about it: *Do you have a lifestyle of gratitude? Who can you encourage? Take the time to encourage one person each day this week.*

_____

_____

_____

NOT YET COMPETENT

David Wakerley is a kids pastor from Hillsong Church in Sydney Australia. He is passionate about children, the generations and leadership that makes a difference.
hillsongkidsbig.com

By taking on this tremendous task of serving the kids of your church, you have received an opportunity.

Check out what Jesus got his disciples to do:

Firstly, Jesus gave his followers the opportunity to do what he did. Everything Jesus was asking them to do they had seen him do time and time again; there were no hidden surprises. But this was not just an object lesson where Jesus expects them to fail and come back with their tails between their legs, saying, "I don't know how you do it Jesus. You're awesome. I could never be like you."

I don't see Jesus setting anyone up for terrible failure. His disciples had a lot to learn, and I guarantee they did not do as well as Jesus on their first outings, but our New Testament wouldn't exist if they hadn't succeeded.

"Very truly I tell you, whoever believes in me will do the works I have been doing, and they will do even greater things than these, because I am going to the Father." John 14:12 (NIV)

Your Church wouldn't exist if the church hadn't spread to every corner of the earth, and believe me; you aren't going to be one to bring that remarkable growth to an end.

Thinking back to my Bible College career, not every assignment was successful. I received a N.Y.C. (Not Yet Competent), on more than one occasion. But just like those lecturers, Jesus can handle my incompetence, and he didn't set me up to fail.

He hasn't set you up to fail, either.

Now He called the twelve together and gave them
POWER and **AUTHORITY**
over all the demons, and the power to heal
diseases. And He sent them out to proclaim the
kingdom of God and to perform healing. And
He said to them, "Take nothing for your journey,
neither a staff, nor a bag, nor bread, nor money;
and do not even have two tunics. And whatever
house you enter, stay there until you leave that
city. And as for all who do not receive you, when
you leave that city, shake the dust off your feet
as a testimony against them." And as they were
leaving, they began going throughout the villages,
**PREACHING
THE GOSPEL**
and healing everywhere.
-Luke 9:1-6

Think about it: *What opportunities has God given you? Are you letting the fear of failure keep you from the next thing God has planned for you?*

_____

_____

_____

_____

_____

_____

FUN & FOUNDATIONS

Amber Pike is the editor of KidzMatter Magazine, an author, a children's minister, and a momma whose passion is to see kids loving the Word of God and walking with Him!
www.amberpike.org

"Are we going to play a game?" I get that question at least once per class from one little boy. (And I'm sure you do, too!) Kids want to have fun. They are geared for fun. They learn from fun.

Kidmin should be fun!

They are kids, after all.

So, how fun are your lessons? Are you engaging a variety of learning styles and smarts, reaching the maximum amount of kids, while having short segments (to keep kids engaged), and adding in elements of fun? (Yeah, that's a lot for a one-hour lesson. No one said kidmin was easy!) These are things that you need to be doing. You need to add in the fun. There should be games in your ministry. Excitement and laughter, that should be a standard.

But a fun ministry isn't all you need. You need a strong foundation.

When you have a fun and exciting activity planned for the boys and girls, one you know they will love, ask yourself, "What is the purpose of this?" Yeah. I'm one of those people that thinks fun needs a purpose. Sometimes, fun for the sake of fun is the purpose. But in ministry, we have been entrusted with precious few hours to speak the truths of God's Word to these boys and girls. Some of them will hear about the saving love of Jesus for the very first (or maybe only) time.

Are you using your hour well?

Yes, fun is important. Give kids a strong foundation by making sure your ministry is built on a strong foundation. Remember the wise and foolish builder? In order to see a strong foundation in the kids you minister to, your ministry needs to be based on the Word. Base your ministry and your lessons on the Word of God… and make it fun!

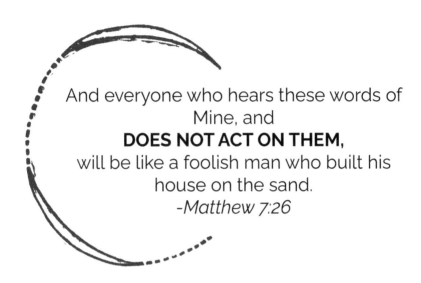

And everyone who hears these words of Mine, and
DOES NOT ACT ON THEM,
will be like a foolish man who built his house on the sand.
-Matthew 7:26

Think about it: *Evaluate your lessons and your ministry. Is your ministry built on the foundation of Christ? Is it fun? What changes do you need to make to see strong foundations in the lives of boys and girls?*

_____
_____
_____
_____
_____
_____

WHERE IS GOD AT 2 DEGREES?

***Amy Goble** is a children's pastor in Dallas, TX. She loves encouraging other kids pastors, Mexican food, and all things glitter.*

I walked outside to find my Pastor installing sealant around the walls of our nursery building. "We gotta take care of our babies" he said.

The nursery had been flooding every time it rained for weeks and try as we might, we couldn't fix it yet.

This time, he was trying something new. He had a new sealant he was installing. "I know what happened to the last seal." He said. "It said on the package it wouldn't last if it was colder than 10°."

We both laughed... because this is Texas! You know what things are normally like in Texas? HOT. Under any regular circumstances, we would totally disregard a "less than 10°" warning as irrelevant. Then "Snowmageddon" happened. Our mild winters turned into 6 inches of snow and temperatures as low as 2°.

That's why the seal didn't work - it was 2 degrees outside.

It can feel that way in life sometimes. We prefer mild winters, balmy summers, and calm waters. Then something happens to test the seal and brings up the question: Where is God?

In October my Dad passed away. Then right before Christmas, one my fellow staff members lost their son in a fatal car accident.

So where was God in the midst of all of this? And where was God at 2 degrees?

My favorite passage of Scripture is Psalm 23:4.

> *Even though I walk*
> *through the darkest valley,*
> *I will fear no evil,*
> *for you are with me;*

Did you see that? The Psalmist is saying that when he walks through the darkest valley there is no need to be afraid because: God is With Me

If I were walking into a fight and knew I would lose - I'd be scared. Now what if I walked into that same fight with a champion? What if I knew I wasn't alone?

It reminds me that I am walking into every single minute of my life with the God of the Universe: A Champion. A Hero...By my Side. I AM NOT ALONE.

Here is my challenge for you: When you have days when it's hard, when you have days when it feels like everything is freezing, pause to remember you have a champion by your side - you are not alone.

And remember to seal the outside of your nursery building - it matters!!

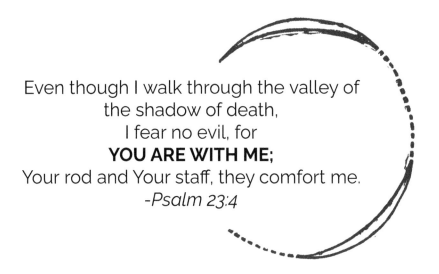

Even though I walk through the valley of
the shadow of death,
I fear no evil, for
YOU ARE WITH ME;
Your rod and Your staff, they comfort me.
-*Psalm 23:4*

Pray about it: *Take time to talk with Jesus today. No matter what you are going through, remember that you are not alone!*

_____

_____

_____

THE CREATIVITY CHALLENGE

Beth Frank loves Jesus, her hubs, her three girls, and thinking creatively. Beth is the co-founder of KidzMatter. She also owns a design company called B Frank Design Co. She was inspired by her oldest daughter's autism diagnosis to write the book Ausomely Blessed.

I believe that all people are created with the ability to think creatively!! I love hanging out with Kidmin people because they are some of the most creative, inspiring, and wild-idea generating people that I have ever met!! But occasionally, I do come into contact with individuals that say they just aren't creative. I just can't accept that. Just like with all higher-level thinking, idea generation and creativity are skills that need to be developed over time. Yes, it is true that some have been gifted by God with a unique, abundant amount of creativity. But let's not let that discourage the rest of us. Here is a checklist of questions to guide your thought process next time you need that next BIG idea.

Am I plugged into my power source for creativity? Nothing, and I do mean nothing will squelch the creative thought process like being disconnected from my creative source, Jesus.

As we all know, our horizontal effectiveness is only as strong as our vertical relationship. For the busy kidmin, this means setting aside strategic time each week where we ourselves can recharge and spiritually renew. Don't forget the key to it all is His new work in us each day. We can't creatively make plans if we haven't first surrendered our life, plans and day to His leadership and leading.

When faced with a challenge, ask yourself "am I asking myself the right questions?". Sometimes when we can't see our way around the problem to a solution it helps to ask a few questions, but they have to be the right questions. Peel back the expected answers and solutions, and strip away the preconceived ideas we have because we have seen other ministries run successfully in a certain way. Look at the heart of the issue and what the ultimate goal is. Sometimes, the most unexpected answers come when we focus on the ultimate goal and not the problem itself.

Pray, pray, and pray. What we need is more of God's anointing and power and less of our man-made, generated, forced ideas. Let him lead and don't be stressed by rushing to meet deadlines. He will provide us the answers we need and prayer is the pipeline He will use.

Get out of the office!!! You know what, for you, is your "zone". Maybe it's an afternoon spent hiking, or maybe it's a little retail therapy, or maybe taking a break and reading from an amazing publication like KidzMatter Magazine. Find time and break away to do whatever it is that fills your creativity meter. Don't feel guilty about this time away, it is imperative for you to develop as a creative leader.

DO NOT COMPARE. I believe comparison is the thief of joy and creativity. Don't look at others and think you need to exactly duplicate. Yes, we need to look at others and learn, but what works successfully for other leaders and ministries might not for us.

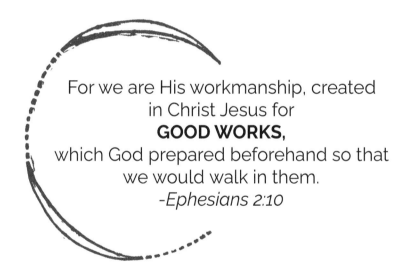

For we are His workmanship, created
in Christ Jesus for
GOOD WORKS,
which God prepared beforehand so that
we would walk in them.
-Ephesians 2:10

Do something about it: Look at the ministry God has called you to and stayed plugged in to Him and His word, ask the right questions, pray, get some personal time charging your creative juices, and let God do the rest. He has some amazing things planned that will blow your mind! Go be creative!!!

_____

_____

_____

STAY IN THE WORD... AND ON YOUR KNEES

Judy Frank serves the kidmin world as Kidmin Academy Support. She is also Ryan's mother, Beth's mother-in-law and Grandma Judy to their 3 beautiful girls. She is also grandma to 5 additional extraordinary little people. Judy reads and responds to each of the students' monthly assignments in Kidmin Academy and is blessed to pray for each student by name during their year in the academy.

A few years ago when Ryan asked me if I would be interested in reading and responding to the Kidmin Academy monthly assignments, I said yes (mostly to be closer to Ryan and Beth and to have a tiny part in their ministry) I had not realized that by reading their assignments and praying for each student that God would beautifully bind my heart to these students. I also didn't realize that as I read their assignments, it would begin to give me a glimpse into each of their lives and ministries, and I was able to see first hand WHY God has chosen EACH of them for kids ministry.

These past few years have been a reminder to me that at any age and in any season of our lives, even when our motives at first are a bit sketchy... if we approach each ministry opportunity with an open heart, God can bless us in incredible ways by divine connections with amazing brothers and sisters in Christ who we would have never known had He not opened the door.

My past 40 years have been filled with having a small business and volunteering at a counseling ministry. God put in my heart a deep compassion for hurting people. I love raising and loving my kids and 8 incredible grandkids, and helping my sweet mom who is now in her late 80s.

I have been saved and serving the Lord since I was a teenager. Yet in 2020, at age 62, underneath the surface was a crippling deep-seated fear from my childhood that left me scarred beyond what seemed possible to completely heal from. God's Word tells us, *"The things that are impossible with people are possible with God,"* Luke 18:27 NASB.

God lifted the fear off of me... just as if a huge boulder was lifted off of my spirit. I don't know how God did it. For most of my adult life, I stayed in the Word and on my knees... "*I sought the Lord and He answered me, and rescued me from all my fears,*" Psalm 34:4 NASB.

So, today at 63 years old, I am finally experiencing a freedom in Christ in a way I have never known before. I need to say to each of you in kids ministry, you may be a leader saved and serving, yet still have a broken piece from past pain. You may be ministering to a child who walks into your class at church who is broken like I was for so many years and needs to find the freedom that only comes through Christ.

So, I am encouraging you my brothers and sisters in Christ to press into His presence, STAY IN THE WORD and ON YOUR KNEES, so that you can continue to speak Jesus into these little people and plant seeds that last for eternity. We must go further than praying a prayer of salvation with each child. We must reach out with deep compassion to the broken and wounded kids and adults to clearly show them that we serve a God who is BIG enough to heal even our deepest pain and turn that pain into purpose, so that these little people can use their testimony like you are to reach a lost and broken world...one child at a time.

...and they **OVERCAME** him because of the blood of the lamb and because of the word of their testimony. *-Revelation 12:11*

Do something about it: Make a plan for this week. When will you have quiet time with the Lord? Make it a priority.

_____

_____

_____

GOD OF MAKING NEW THINGS

***Andy Ye** is the founder and director of Ertongshigong.com, a children's minister, and a father of two daughters whose passion is to reach the hearts of the next generation in his culture!*
andy@ertongshigong.com

In 2014, we started our children's ministry on a social app in China. This was because children's ministry was way more neglected and overlooked here.

On a daily basis and all year round, we have been posting all kinds of kidmin related resources, and gradually our social account became one of the leading and most influential kidmin in our country.

Six years later, the restriction of internet in our country got more and more intense. Our account was shut down and blocked permanently because of so-called "forbidden" contents teaching the good news to kids under eighteen years old. All of a sudden, we lost all our connection with our followers, and couldn't send anything out directly. At the same time, my wife was diagnosed with cancer and had surgery. She used to lead workshops to train Sunday school teachers. Now both ministries had to stop.

When we tried to seek his will, He reminded us of Isaiah 43:19. Yes, the ministry is HIS ministry; the followers and kids are HIS people! Since this door was closed, he must open another door for us. And it must be a bigger one!

Early before the breakout of Covid-19, we used ZOOM to have meetings with our coworkers. So why don't we take more advantage of ZOOM? We began to start online Sunday school classes and online VBS on ZOOM. It has been great.

We got opportunities to directly minister to those kids who are not allowed to go to churches and even some non-church kids. In the latest online VBS, we got a chance to work with 80+ churches and groups from all over the country, ministering to over 900 children.

We also began to organize online training instead of workshops. In 2020, we organized eight online classes, one after another, nonstop. As a result, over 300 Sunday school teachers were equipped in one year. My wife often joked that she never thought as a cancer patient in her recovery time, she could do a lot more than when she was healthy. That's something only our God could do!

If you are experiencing some tough and challenging situation in your ministry, remember it's time for HIM to do a new thing in your life. It might be your personal growth, or some breakthrough in your ministry.

Never be discouraged or lose heart! The God we are serving is the God of doing new things.

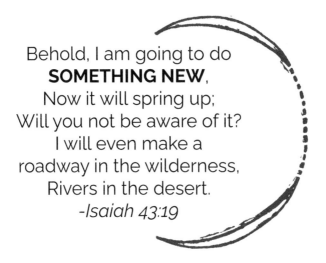

Behold, I am going to do
SOMETHING NEW,
Now it will spring up;
Will you not be aware of it?
I will even make a
roadway in the wilderness,
Rivers in the desert.
-*Isaiah 43:19*

Pray about it: *Identify and acknowledge God's grace in your present life and ministry. If you are experiencing a hard time, submit yourself into God's hand and ask him to show you how he would glorify himself through you and your ministry.*

_____

_____

_____

CHOOSE YOUR FOCUS

Jan Hanson is the Kids & Families Director at FCC Napa (California). She began serving in kids' ministry as a volunteer. God opened doors that led to church staff roles, for a combined 18 years, where she continues to discover a passion to encourage and resource parents and volunteers to help kids grow an everyday faith.

My family and my husband's have taken countless photos over many years. We continued the tradition... photos of our kids growing up, birthdays, vacations, forced poses, silly candid shots, you name it. One problem with photos from our own childhoods is they are slides. (Yes, I just dated myself.) We have some great tools to view and save slides and have old printed photos digitized. Some have been damaged over the years, but other programs can touch up and restore the photos.

There's one type of photo that cannot be corrected though... photos that are out of focus. You can't make a blurry photo unblurry. You can squint and guess at whose faces they are, but you can't change them to make it clear. Thankfully, today we can instantly see photos we take with our phones... and then call for a do-over if needed!

I realized something while looking at some of those old, blurry photos. Because the photographer focused on something other than the main subject, it caused the main subject to become out of focus. Have you noticed, especially since March 2020, we've done that? Not with photos, but with our ministry to kids and families. And if we're being honest, at times, even our personal lives. If we're focused on the wrong things, it can blur our vision, then shift us away from what should be our main ministry focus ... helping kids know Jesus and discover their place in God's story.

We get to choose our focus every day. As people called to be light and encouragement to families with kids, we have the privilege of partnering with parents. We get to be instrumental in guiding them to bring Jesus into their daily lives by encouraging them to "think about such things".

Has it been easy or without battle wounds as we've prayed, called, emailed, texted, dropped off, showed up, posted, zoomed, penned, cried, cheered, learned, planned, encouraged, and so much more? Not at all. But it's been true, noble, right, pure, lovely, admirable, and praiseworthy.

Choose your focus. Keep thinking about such things. Because you are not only doing those things, you ARE those things to Father God.

Finally, brothers and sisters,
whatever is true,
whatever is honorable,
whatever is right,
whatever is pure,
whatever is lovely,
whatever is commendable,
if there is any excellence and if anything
worthy of praise,
THINK ABOUT THESE THINGS.
-Philippians 4:8

Pray about it: *How's your focus? Spend some time with the Lord. Ask him to adjust your focus.*

_____

_____

_____

_____

_____

_____

ONE PERSON AT A TIME

Beth Frank loves Jesus, her hubs, her three girls, and thinking creatively. Beth is the co-founder of KidzMatter. She also owns a design company called B Frank Design Co. She was inspired by her oldest daughter's autism diagnosis to write the book Ausomely Blessed.

I think as leaders and kidmin people we think of "outreach" as something large scale. How many visitors can we bring in through this year's VBS? What amazing, creative idea can we come up with for our Easter outreach this year? I'm all for large-scale, creative ways to reach those outside of our church building, but for today I want to focus on the seemingly small idea of personal outreach.

Who has God called me to, personally, this week? What are my personal God assignments for the day?

If we look at the life of Jesus, He did large-scale ministry to the masses, but He also emphasized one-on-one relationships. In Luke 15, we read the parable of the lost sheep. Jesus left the masses to go after the one. Jesus was reminding us of the importance of seeking one - just one. Jesus reached thousands through His earthly ministry, but spent lots of time investing individually in the twelve.

On Sunday nights, I've made it a habit to sit quietly (I'll confess, I do this during church sometimes) and ask God to place a few people on my heart for the coming week. I pray and wait for the assignments that God will give to me. I usually jot these down somewhere so I don't forgot, although this is an unnecessary step because once God speaks to me about someone, he usually keeps after me until I respond! I used to be overwhelmed by the needs around me and felt powerless in the face of those demands, but God has shown me that it isn't an "all or nothing" approach. I don't need to provide a theological dissertation to someone who has been diagnosed with cancer on why God allows suffering. I just need to show love.

Usually, my list includes things like taking someone a meal, sending a card or asking someone out for coffee. This isn't hard stuff and doesn't require huge amounts of time or planning, I just need to take the time and be strategic about reaching out to those in my church and community that God has placed on my heart. Remember that while you are called to be a leader and do large-scale outreach, it's just as important to do ministry one-on-one.

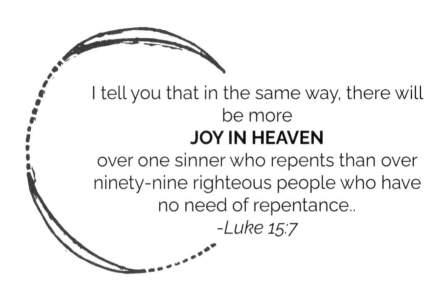

I tell you that in the same way, there will be more
JOY IN HEAVEN
over one sinner who repents than over ninety-nine righteous people who have no need of repentance..
-Luke 15:7

***Pray about it:** Ask God to give you a list of appointments for the week. He will... and he will amaze you with the opportunities and blessings that come from being willing to show his love and grace in small tangible ways to those around you.*

_____

_____

_____

YOU'RE BEING WATCHED

Ryan Frank is a pastor, publisher, and entrepreneur. He serves as CEO of KidzMatter, co-founder of KidzMatter Mega-Con, and CEO of Frank Insurance Agency. Ryan and his wife, Beth, run several businesses and love to travel and spend time with their three daughters.
ryanfrank.com

I'm writing this as I sit in the Hard Rock Stadium in Miami, Florida, the home of the Miami Dolphins. Whenever this football team gathers to play, more than 38,000 people get together and watch a handful of people on the field throwing a football.

I want to encourage you with a leadership thought today. 38,000 people gather, and they watch some people play on the field. Every day there are people that are watching you. Did you know that?

As a leader, people are watching you all the time. They're not just watching you when you're on the stage. They're not just watching you when you're doing your thing. They are watching your expressions. They are watching the way you walk into the office. They are watching the way that you talk to your spouse and to your kids. They are watching the way that you handle conflict. They are watching the way that you present yourself on social media.

Now, if that alarms you, it shouldn't. It should actually be a wake-up call because all of us, as leaders, are "on" all the time.

How are your expressions, your attitude, or your conversations? How are you responding during the good days and during the bad days? It really, really matters. The people that follow you, the people that listen to you, the people that lead with you, they really care about you. As they watch you, they are determining IF you are someone they can trust. Are you someone that has credibility? Are you someone that they want to follow?

Be someone worth following. Be someone worth influencing. Be someone worth the credibility that you desire.

People are watching you every day. There may not be 38,000 people in a stadium watching you, but there are eyeballs watching you every day. It may just be a few, but those few matter! So, remember to be the person that God's called you to be. Live the life that you know you want to live, and pursue your dreams along the way.

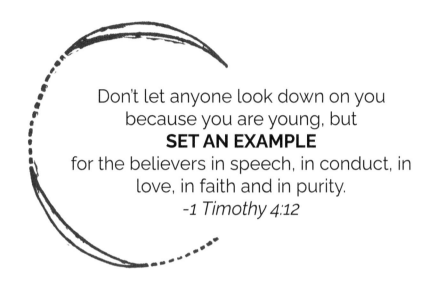

Don't let anyone look down on you because you are young, but
SET AN EXAMPLE
for the believers in speech, in conduct, in love, in faith and in purity.
-1 Timothy 4:12

Think about it: *What do people see when they watch you? Are you someone worth following?*

_____

_____

_____

LOVE THAT GOES BEYOND?

Esther Moreno is an author and speaker. She is the founder of Child's Heart which is dedicated to equipping children's ministry leaders to reach children and families.
www.childsheart83.com

I will never forget that one child. You know who I'm talking about. That one kid who just gets under your skin. I don't care how long you've been in children's ministry or how much you love working with kids. Everyone has that one child and if you haven't had yours yet, just keep working in children's ministry. Some people call them the troublemakers, rebel rousers, or my personal favorite: distractor of all things good after laboring for a whole week trying to perfect a lesson! Whew! That was a mouthful. Well, I had mine and her name was Julie.

Julie was a master at the pouty face. She questioned and complained about everything! She threw major fits when she didn't get her way, and let's not talk about her scream. Her screech could reach an astronaut's ears if they were on the moon! I will never forget when Julie was assigned to my group for the season. Every Wednesday I would tense up when I realized it was time for mid-week programming. I began to worry less about the lesson and more about what problems Julie would cause for me that evening. Like so many other children's ministry leaders, I experienced a lapse in judgement and forgot what it was all about.

Praise God for the gentle nudge of the Holy Spirit. It got my mind back where it was supposed to be. God had reminded me that it wasn't about flawlessly executing everything I had planned. It wasn't about maintaining the perfect peaceful environment. It wasn't even about Julie's irate behavior. Despite her stubborn attitude, God reminded me that it was all about him. My role was to reveal him to Julie by simply loving her through the good, the bad, and the ugly.

As you may have guessed, it wasn't long after my epiphany when Julie's inner grizzly bear had showed up during mid-week programming. Only this time was different. After vehemently refusing to go back into the classroom following a group bathroom break, Julie hunkered down behind a cabinet. With all my nerves intact, I told Julie that I loved her and that sometimes I have bad days too, but that I was so happy she still showed up today. Julie looked up, wiped her crocodile tears, and moved from behind the cabinet. I experienced a breakthrough that day with Julie, which led to a strong bond and many unwarranted hugs, all because I decided to act on God's love instead of my own way.

Children's Ministry leader, God has called for us to not only teach kids about him, but to demonstrate his love by how we respond to them. How do you handle kids that get under your skin? How can you respond next time in a way that reveals God's love to them? If you're feeling frustrated with a child, ask God to help you see them the way He does and to cultivate a love for them that extends beyond their difficult behavior.

Love is
PATIENT,
love is
KIND.
-1 Corinthians 13:4a

Do something about it: Share God's love with THAT child this week.

_____

_____

_____

WHERE WERE YOU?

Amber Pike is the editor of KidzMatter Magazine, an author, a children's minister, and a momma whose passion is to see kids loving the Word of God and walking with Him!
www.amberpike.org

Growing up, my mom was our church's VBS director, and she had a distinct style of leading, that at the time, I didn't love. If she signed up for something, I was signed up for it as well. She would hand off VBS tasks to me and just let me handle them. She knew I was capable, and instead of micromanaging me, she let me learn how to do them.

While that was excellent training for the ministry, at the time, I was less than enthusiastic about being "volunt-told" to help. But as I sit back and reflect on my VBS training, as well as dozens and dozens of other things from my life, I can't help but marvel at God's sovereignty.

It's like he knew I would need that VBS training. It's like, in his infinite wisdom, he knew that I would go into the ministry. It's like he knew exactly what I would need later in life, like he had a plan.

We know of course that God does have a plan for our futures, and a good plan at that. But we can't always see or understand his plans. [During my VBS helping days, I'm pretty sure I was still planning on being a country music star, not a children's ministry leader.] And when we don't realize his plans for our life, we start to question. "Why God?"

Job did. This man of God had almost his entire life, ripped away from him. He didn't see God's plan, so he asked God why.

Then God answered.

"Where were you?"

I love that part of Job. God basically tells Job that he alone is God, the creator of the universe, and if he could do all of those amazing things (things that are more than our human brains can even fathom), Job needed to trust that God was still in control of his life.

Do you need to trust God a little bit more? He is still in control of your life, even when things seem crazy or like they are falling apart. God is in control when life is going great and when you just aren't sure what is going on. Through the good days and the not so good, God is still in control. And he has a plan for your life and your ministry, even when it doesn't seem like it.

Where were
you when
I laid the
earth's foundations?
-Job 38:4

Think about it: *"Where were you?" Take some time and think about our amazing God, the controller and creator of the universe. Ask yourself, is there anything out of His control?*

_____

_____

_____

_____

COVERING THE NEXT GENERATION

Abram Gomez is the Senior Executive Pastor of Cross Church, a multisite church located in the Rio Grande Valley of Texas. He has a passion for leadership and helps to equip leaders.
www.abramgomez.com

"You are going to be a preacher."

Those were the final words my grandmother spoke to me right before her passing in 1996. I was 17 at the time, two years prior to actually receiving from the Lord a calling to preach his Word. Unbeknownst to me, my grandmother was covering me with her prophetic words and prayers.

Truthfully, I wasn't even serving the Lord at the age of 17. I didn't have the appearance of one called to preach, by my own opinion. I actually had plans to go into the medical field.

It's amazing how an older generation can cover the next generation through their words, good works, and spiritual engagement. You really do help to make a difference in the lives of so many young hearts.

Throughout the Bible, we see this time and time again. Jacob did it with his sons. Moses did it with his leaders. Mordecai did it with Esther.

Every year, Hannah would make a robe for her son Samuel. I am pretty sure she didn't make it according to the size he was, but to where he was going and growing. It never failed. A robe exchange always occurred around the time that they would offer the yearly sacrifice. And for the following year, Samuel would walk in the covering of his mother.

Think about that for a moment: what Hannah did, Samuel walked in.

Right now, there is a generation that is in need of covering. They are walking around without someone's prayers, guidance, and affirmation. No one has told them about the things of God. No one has told them that there is a special purpose for their life. No one has taken time to pull out the potential the Lord has already placed within him or her. We could blame or we could become. The Lord has called you for such a time as this to help provide the covering.

The enemy would love to keep them uncovered, but the Lord has a counter plan by sending you into the field. You have been equipped with the right spiritual weapons to fight for a generation and the Lord's anointing is upon you.

The next time you walk into your group, classroom, or church, remember we cover because we are covered by His grace.

Now Samuel was ministering before the Lord, as a boy wearing a linen ephod. And his mother would make for him a little robe and bring it up to him from year to year when she would come up with her husband to offer the yearly sacrifice.
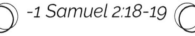 *-1 Samuel 2:18-19*

Think about it: What are some practical ways you think you could help provide covering for students? What has helped you in your personal walk with the Lord?

_____

_____

_____

FAITH OVER FEAR

Beth Frank loves Jesus, her hubs, her three girls, and thinking creatively. Beth is the co-founder of KidzMatter. She also owns a design company called B Frank Design Co. She was inspired by her oldest daughter's autism diagnosis to write the book Ausomely Blessed.

As we are prayerfully approaching the final stages of a global pandemic, I find myself looking back over the past year and a half that has been difficult in about every way. I'm sure for most of us, the pandemic left us dealing with unprecedented challenges. When Ryan and I have conversations with friends and other ministry leaders from across the world, it is always sobering for me to realize the individual struggles this time in history has brought. Life recently has been hard, and ministry life challenges have increased exponentially.

I will be honest and admit that a lot of days this past year, I had the thought and desire to just quit. I just didn't want to face the complexity of it anymore. I'm sure if we were sitting down over coffee to have a heart to heart that you might admit the same thing. During any given day this last year, we have faced struggles that caused our hearts to feel fear, frustration, anxiety, anger, and possibly even hopelessness. No, a global pandemic hasn't been easy for most.

BUT, we serve a big God, who understands our struggles and walks with us through them. Hebrews 4:15-16 says *"For we do not have a high priest who cannot sympathize with our weaknesses, but One who has been tempted in all things just as we are, yet without sin. Therefore let's approach the throne of grace with confidence, so that we may receive mercy and find grace for help at the time of our need."* Scripture is filled with verses that say something like "take courage, for I am with you". I don't think this is a mistake at all. God knew that we as believers living here on earth would need a constant reminder that He is in fact right here with us.

This week as I was driving in my car feeling very overwhelmed and discouraged, I was listening to worship music to try and give my struggles to the One who can handle them. I felt a gentle whisper in my soul. Jesus kindly reminded me, that yes, he is with me and that I was forgetting that he is enough. I've grown up in church, I know to say all the platitudes and yes, Jesus is always with us. But he quietly paused all my anxious thoughts in the car that day with going beyond my platitudes with the gentle but firm reminder that he will always be enough for whatever I bring him. Even if everything my human heart worries about catastrophically comes true, he is still enough for that.

Friend, what struggle do you need to be reminded of today that God is enough to handle even that? Start by reading through Hebrews 11 specifically thinking about what was promised but had not been yet seen. Faith isn't faith if we are living with all promises fulfilled. Hebrews 11:13 reminds us that those in the verses before died without seeing the promises, but they had seen them from afar which caused them to live as strangers or exiles here on earth.

You and I are promised that Jesus is enough for whatever we are facing. We may not understand the trial, we may not be able to trace God's plan currently, but we can stand confidently in faith as children of promise. No, the pandemic did not make us feel at home here on this planet, but that's a good thing. It's good to remember that we need to look forward and welcome the promises from a distance.

Let's commit together to not quitting, not getting discouraged, not feeling hopeless, and not giving in to fear. Let's live in faith and trust Jesus is enough for whatever the future brings our way. I am cheering you on!

For we do not have a high priest who cannot sympathize with our weaknesses, but One who has been tempted in all things just as we are, yet without sin. Therefore let's approach the throne of grace with confidence, so that we may receive mercy and find grace for help at the time of our need.
-Hebrews 4:15-16

Think about it: *Where are you feeling hopelessness or discouragement, today? When those feelings strike, remind yourself that Jesus is enough for whatever is going on in your life (or the world).*

_____

_____

_____

WHAT'S IN YOUR POCKET?

Arlene Pellicane is a speaker, host of the Happy Home podcast, and author of several books including Parents Rising and Screen Kids. You can meet her family in the documentary Screen Kids: In Their Own Words.
www.ArlenePellicane.com
www.HappyHomeUniversity.com/film

One afternoon, I was going through the laundry, checking all the pockets before loading the washing machine. I found something I had never found before in one my kid's pant pockets: silly putty. I was very relieved I didn't find out what that sticky, bouncy, elastic substance would do to the other clothes in the wash!

Another item pulled out of my pocket made me smile. It was a receipt for puppy toys. We had just got our first pet, a cute brown dog who was getting bigger by the second. I pulled play money from my daughter's pocket from church. These colorful bucks were earned by bringing a Bible or offering.

In each pocket, I found evidence of where we had been, what we had done, and what we valued enough to keep (or what we forgot to throw away!). In the hidden, quiet place of the laundry room, I sorted the items. Silly putty would go back to my child. Play money and doggie toy receipt went to the trash.

You know, sometimes we need to check the "pockets" of our lives in a quiet place. What would the evidence found in our pockets, purses and homes say about our faith?

Is there anything we're holding on to that should be thrown away? Perhaps it's a grudge or insecurity.

Are there places we are going or activities we're involved with that aren't healthy for us?

What do our receipts say about our financial stewardship?

Perhaps we could use a few moments today to de-clutter our pockets, asking God for wisdom in life. The true way to a beautiful home isn't found in an interior decorating magazine or purchasing lovely furniture on credit. Today's verse from Proverbs 24 tells us that rare and beautiful treasures are results of living with wisdom, understanding, and knowledge.

King Solomon asked God for wisdom; for a discerning heart to distinguish between right and wrong (1 Kings 3:9). Likewise, we can ask God for carefulness and shrewdness to manage the daily matters of our lives and ministries.

Pay attention to the details of your life because they are shaping your life's story. Maybe your phone is taking too much prominence, your treasured possession in your pocket or purse. We don't want to build our lives on technology, but on Christ alone.

Take time to empty out your pockets, making sure there isn't anything hidden in your life which needs to be surrendered to God. Throw away what ensnares you and extra clutter that weighs you down. Build your home on wisdom, understanding, and knowledge. And always remove the silly putty before you do the laundry!

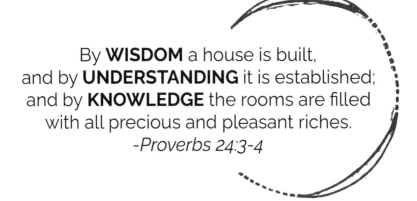

By **WISDOM** a house is built,
and by **UNDERSTANDING** it is established;
and by **KNOWLEDGE** the rooms are filled
with all precious and pleasant riches.
-Proverbs 24:3-4

Talk about it: *What is one area in your life where you need more power and strength, God's wisdom and knowledge? Talk about this with a spiritual mentor or godly friend in your life.*

_____

_____

_____

EARTHEN VESSELS

__Karen Bishir__, a retired Family and Consumer Science teacher, is the interim children's director at Liberty Baptist Church, Sweetser, Indiana, where her husband, Terry, serves as pastor. She is involved with the women's ministry, Awana, and the music ministry. She is mother to four married children and "mamie" to thirteen grandkids.

Children's ministry would be virtually impossible without the assistance of a wonderful team of volunteers. As I stroll through our children's center each Sunday morning, Sunday evening, and Thursday night, I am reminded of this. I was very focused on this fact this past month as we experienced VBS and then kids' camp. Our volunteer servant leaders are invaluable. These individuals are indeed treasures.

Yet, according to 2 Corinthians 4:7, the treasure is contained in earthen containers. We are the earthen containers. These containers were clay pots. They were cheap and often flawed. They were, however, necessary in the lives of individuals in Paul's day. Paul saw himself as an old, clay pot. He was expendable and he was without perfection.

God, himself, is the treasure. It is his glory. It is his power that overcomes our weaknesses and offers salvation to us. Despite our frailty and insufficiency, God uses these earthen containers. As we see in this passage, Christ becomes more visible as a result of our weaknesses.

I do so appreciate our team of kids' workers. There are those who serve as family units. There are single moms and single dads. There are teens who love Jesus, serving, and kids. There are faithful co-workers who battle constant physical pain or are deeply concerned about loved ones and their spiritual battles. Each volunteer has a story to tell as to how God has equipped them, in spite of their frailties, and is able to shine through their lives.

How I love building relationships with this great team. We share the common goal of loving these children who have been placed into our lives. Just remember, we become a more valuable tool in God's tool chest BECAUSE of our difficulties and God is glorified.

The following list describes many of my co-laborers: faithful, true to the Word, examples of Christ, love for Jesus, kids, and other leaders, followers, welcoming, friendly, organized, life-long learners, Spirit-filled and Spirit-led, punctual, wise stewards, evangelistic, prayer warriors, holy living, flexible, wise, and best of all – clay pots.

But we have this treasure in earthen containers, so that the extraordinary greatness of the power will be of God and not from ourselves; we are afflicted in every way, but **NOT CRUSHED;** perplexed, but **NOT DESPAIRING**; persecuted, but **NOT ABANDONED**; struck down, but **NOT DESTROYED**; always carrying around in the body the dying of Jesus, so that the life of Jesus may also be revealed in our body.
-2 Corinthians 4:7-10

Pray about it: *Are you discouraged in the midst of your difficulties? Do you see God's glory and power shining through you to those you serve?*

_____

_____

_____

_____

KIDS MINISTRY IS FOUNDATIONAL

Julie Crawford lives in Ontario, Canada and has been a children's pastor for 16 years. She has a passion to see kids come to know, love and serve Jesus as their Lord and Savior. Having herself accepted Christ at the age of 7, she understands how foundational kid's ministry is.

Kid's ministry is foundational!

Can I hear an AMEN?!

More than half of the people that will believe in Jesus do so by age 12. By the time a child is 10, their basic moral foundation has been formed as well as their basic beliefs about the nature of God, & the everlasting love of Jesus. There is a season in a person's life when they are most open to learning what it means to choose Jesus – it's when they are kids

We have a huge responsibility before us that should not be taken lightly. Each week we get to pour truth into these little hearts and minds when they are most open to it. Sharing the Gospel with some children for the very first time and helping them to form their very first thoughts about who God is – that's what we get to do. We are raising up a future generation of young people that will impact this world for Christ. We only have these kids for a short time, but foundational truths are being poured into them.

How many adult problems would be solved if every kid knew they have a Heavenly Father who loves them? Or, if they knew they can place their trust in Jesus for every area of their lives? If people knew their place in God's story and his plan and purpose for them so much of the world's problems would not exist.

Our mission is to point kids to Jesus. He is the one who draws them. He is the one who saves them. Our job is to be obedient to what he has called us to do and to use our God given talents for his glory. When you love Jesus and love kids-WOW that is a powerful combination and there is no limit to what God can do.

But Jesus said, "Leave the children alone,
and do not forbid them to come to Me;
for the
KINGDOM OF HEAVEN
belongs to such as these."
-Matthew 19:14

Pray about it: *Take a few moments and think back to when God called you into the ministry. What an amazing calling he has placed on your life. Never forget it's importance.*

_____

_____

_____

_____

_____

_____

SMASH 'EM

***Nicole Jones** is the Creative Arts Pastor at Southern Hills, the Church at City Station, located in Carrollton, Georgia. City Station is a community center which also houses a fitness center, preschool, college-student housing, and cafe, all owned and operated by the church.*
sohillscc.com

In typical Israelite fashion, in Numbers 21 we see the recently freed people complaining and grumbling, wishing they were still enslaved back in Egypt. After all He's done for the Israelites, I imagine the Lord is about on His last nerve. God sends serpents into the Israelite camp and many people die from snake bites. The people turn to Moses, repentant and pleading for God to remove the snakes. In response, God instructs Moses to make a bronze serpent and whoever looks at the serpent will be healed from a bite.

Beyond the strangeness of this account, I never really thought much more about the bronze snake. Then this year when he made a second appearance in my Bible reading, I took notice.

In 2 Kings 18, we read about King Hezekiah, who was pleasing in the Lord's sight. Over the years, the people had strayed away from the Lord, following the example of their previous kings and the other nations they intermingled with, despite the Lord's warnings. One of the first things Hezekiah did as King was put a stop to the rampant idol worship in Israel. In 2 Kings 18:4 it says, *"He removed the high places and smashed the memorial stones to pieces, and cut down the Asherah. He also crushed to pieces the bronze serpent that Moses had made, for until those days the sons of Israel had been burning incense to it; and it was called Nehushtan."*

It's been about 750 years since Moses made the bronze serpent. Entire generations have lived and died. Apparently, like the Israelites were known to do, they forgot what God had done. They began to worship the metallic snake, believing it was the thing healing them and not the Lord. This gift from God became an idol.

Don't we do the same? We ask for a job, God provides, and then we allow it to consume us. We pray for children and later worship them as if they were dipped in bronze themselves. We pray, God gives, and then we worship the gift. Luckily, God has not sent any slithering beasts into our homes to remind us of His power (though, we did find a snake skin in our attic recently...), but I know His heart is breaking at our betrayal nonetheless.

And you shall love the Lord your God with all your **HEART** and with all your **SOUL** and with all your **STRENGTH**.
-Deuteronomy 6:5

Pray about it: *Like Hezekiah, are there idols in your life you need to smash? Maybe not literally, but do you need to repent and relinquish the throne of your heart to the Lord again? Where do you need to turn your eyes away from the gift and back to the Great Giver?*

_____

_____

_____

_____

_____

_____

FROM BLESSING TO CURSE

Nicole Jones is the Creative Arts Pastor at Southern Hills, the Church at City Station, located in Carrollton, Georgia. City Station is a community center which also houses a fitness center, preschool, college-student housing, and cafe, all owned and operated by the church.
sohillscc.com

Last week, we revisited the stories in Numbers 21 and 2 Kings 18 about the bronze serpent. The Israelites had turned a gift from the Lord into an idol; but what the chosen people of God are more well known for is their grumbling spirit. In Egypt, they are subjected to backbreaking work and beaten for the slightest offense. Then, God steps in and frees the Israelites in the most miraculous way! Their hearts should be forever grateful as they owe their very lives to the Lord. Yet, as they begin their journey to the Promised Land, they turn into a bunch of hangry toddlers. They long for the days of Egypt when they had meat to eat... and also worked under the relentless sun and unforgiving whip. They would rather die full than free.

Being a good and faithful Father, God gives them mana in the morning and quail in the evening. He even makes water come from a rock! They always have enough and their bellies are full.

But are the people happy? Not for very long.

I must confess, this is my struggle. We prayed for a car and God provided. Years later, I hated the thing. I would have given it away just to be rid of it. My husband reminded me how we prayed for a car and God answered in a way we never expected. I had taken a blessing and made it into a curse.

We've seen this a lot with college graduates, too. They seek the Lord and feel confident they are following his will as they accept a new position. This new journey has them giddy with excitement. Then within months, they grumble and complain, just like the Israelites in the wilderness.

God gave the Israelites a calling and the people made it a burden. Maybe you've done this with your spouse. Maybe it's your ministry. Maybe it's just that you have to eat beans and rice for a season.

While it's easy to point at the Israelites and ask, "How could they miss it after what they witnessed?", we unfortunately are very much the same. Like the Israelites, we owe God our very lives. We should be forever grateful no matter what this life brings! Everything else is just bread from heaven, or gravy as the saying goes.

Do all things without complaining or arguments.
-*Philippians 2:14*

Pray about it: *Are you grumbling about a gift from the Lord? Has he given you a blessing and you made it into a curse? Confess it to God and repent. Ask God to help you rediscover the joy of this gift.*

_____
_____
_____
_____
_____
_____

SUCH A TIME AS THIS

Brittany Nelson is the creator of Deeper KidMin (deeperkidmin.com), a digital hub of creative resources made FOR kidmin leaders BY kidmin leaders. Her other adventures include being a toddler mom, working part-time for her church in an administrative role, reading as many books as she can, volunteering with her husband's youth group, and drinking lots of herbal tea.

Ministry is exhausting. And children's ministry can often bring a whole other level of exhaustion. (There's nothing quite like post-VBS or post-camp tiredness, can I get an amen?)

As a children's ministry leader, you understand what it means to be worn out and weary, and the past couple of years in ministry have thrown extra curveballs and roadblocks your way.

Maybe you're scrambling week to week to find enough volunteers to serve in your ministry and just want to enjoy a Saturday night without being fearful of that late-night-calling-out-sick text.

Maybe you feel like your creativity is spent when it comes to planning for in-person and online events.

Maybe you are wrestling with your own bias and understanding of racial injustice and aren't sure how to equip your families to move toward racial reconciliation too.

Maybe you're exploring family ministry and working hard to convince your staff and senior pastors about the importance of intergenerational discipleship.

Maybe you're just worn out from feeling the pressure to connect with families in new ways, while also trying to figure out what life looks like for your own family.

If no one's told you this lately, you're doing a great job, kidmin leader.

One verse that God has put on my heart and in my mind this season is Esther 4:14...

"... and who knows whether you have not attained royalty for such a time as this?"

God placed Esther in an exhausting and challenging situation so he could use her to save her people. He knew she would be exactly what the situation needed.

You are in your role, at your church, leading your kids and families during this season of ministry for a reason, and God placed you there during this time because he knew you would be exactly what your church needed.

Be encouraged today, friends. I know you're worn down. I know you feel creatively drained. Hang in there. God has led you to your position for such a time as this, and he will continue to be faithful through it.

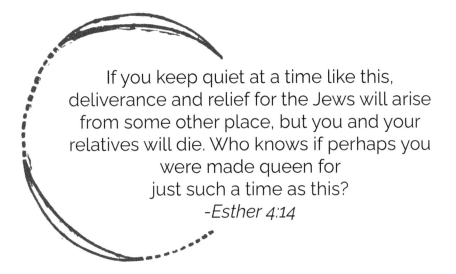

If you keep quiet at a time like this, deliverance and relief for the Jews will arise from some other place, but you and your relatives will die. Who knows if perhaps you were made queen for just such a time as this?
-Esther 4:14

Think about it: *Make a list of 3 things you're grateful for in this season, despite the weariness, and ask God to strengthen you in your role.*

_____

_____

_____

_____

_____

_____

HEARTS ON FIRE

***Josh Zello** is husband to Hannah, father to Avery, and preschool pastor at nineteen:ten church in Boerne, TX. He's passionate about preschoolers, gospel-centered ministry, and crazy socks.*
www.preschoolpastor.com

It's really the goal of every minister.

Don't you want to walk away from your own personal devotion times saying to yourself, "Was my heart not burning within me as I was reading the Scriptures?"

Don't you want the kids in your ministry to walk away every Sunday morning saying to themselves, "Were not our hearts burning within us when the Scriptures were explained to us this morning?"

Jesus shows us how this can happen in Luke 24.

Two people are traveling by foot between Jerusalem and Emmaus. These two had seen extraordinary ministry from Jesus. They had seen Jesus turn water into wine, heal the lame, tell amazing stories, feed crowds with just a little bit of food, give sight to the blind, and even raise people from the dead. But they had also seen tremendous heartbreak. They had seen Jesus be falsely accused, executed in public, and buried in a tomb guarded by soldiers. Hope had left them, for their hope was rooted in their experiences, and not the Word of God.

It's the third day.

Jesus is alive, but they don't believe it. Yet.

Jesus himself approaches them, but their eyes are kept from seeing Him as He is. In a rather funny moment, Jesus implores them to tell them more about Jesus. And they do, but of course, they leave off the best part. Jesus is alive! His story didn't end in death and defeat. His story is continuing in victory!

Jesus takes them to the Scriptures, and shows them how every single Old Testament story pointed to what had to happen in the death and resurrection. Jesus showed them in this moment that if their hope was rooted in the Scriptures (and a Christ-centered approach), then they would know that everything was happening just as it was supposed to. Have hope! Jesus is alive!

When Jesus finally reveals himself, these two are stunned. But their first thought isn't: "Whoa! It's Jesus!" Their first thought is this: "Our hearts burned within us when he showed us that Scripture was all about Jesus!" See, their hope had shifted from being rooted in their experiences to instead being rooted in the Word of God. That changed everything!

They said to one another, "Were our hearts not
BURNING WITHIN US
when He was speaking to us on the road,
while He was explaining the Scriptures to us?"
-Luke 24:32

Think about it: *How do you read Scripture? Do you read Scripture in a way that causes you to know Jesus more? How do you teach Scripture? Do the little people who sit under your teaching walk away with their hearts on fire, and filled with hope in the Gospel of Jesus Christ?*

_____

_____

_____

ENCOURAGE ONE ANOTHER

***Lisa Ware** is a wife, mom, grandma, and a "retired" children's pastor/ director. Her heart is to love God, love her family, love kids, and encourage any fellow ministry folks the Lord puts in her path.*

Ministry is hard. It's personal. And it's often draining.

BUT God!

He knew long before he set you in ministry what you would need—what we all would need—endurance and encouragement! He filled his Word with just that. He sent his Son as an example of just that. Christ Jesus walked before you and me on this ministry journey. Father God put him in place showing us first-hand how to be an encourager.

Jesus reminds us that the Father knows our needs, hears our cries, and loves us so much that he will always take care of us. God wants us to be the encourager Jesus showed us during His earthly ministry.

Being an encourager can be as simple as sending a smiley face or a heart emoji electronically, or as complex as meeting the person for coffee or a meal and being there to listen and pray.

Being an encourager happens when we make the decision to reach out. It's intentional. It doesn't have to rely on how we feel or where we are personally—it can actually lift our mood in the process!

The second part of Romans 15:5 is a prayer that we would be of the same attitude of mind towards each other. Encouraging another person (or persons) will do just that—and that brings glory to God!

What if you are the one needing encouragement, you say? Share where you are with someone you know will be your support. Oftentimes, we hum along living our lives and even those closest to us don't know we are feeling down. God reminds us in Matthew chapter 7 that we are to ASK-SEEK-KNOCK!

Dear Heavenly Father, thank you for knowing what I need even before I need it. Thank you for encouraging me all throughout your Word. Help me to be an encourager, just as Christ Jesus demonstrated. Help me to hear your voice nudging me to encourage another. Give me the words and actions when I may not know what to say or do. Amen.

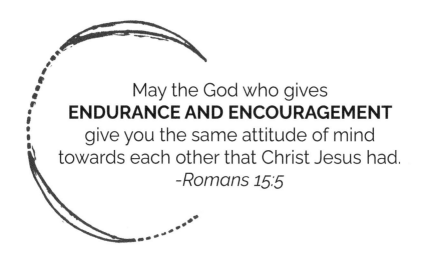

May the God who gives
ENDURANCE AND ENCOURAGEMENT
give you the same attitude of mind
towards each other that Christ Jesus had.
-*Romans 15:5*

Pray about it: *Who is God laying on your heart to encourage? Who has God put in your path that needs encouragement?*

_____

_____

_____

PHASES OF LIFE

Amy Bates *is a long-time children's director, and excited about learning new things. She is loving the second phase of her life with her husband and grown children, whom she loves to spend time with when they can organize their busy schedules together!*

Recently, I spent time with a dear friend from my early married life. We met at church and connected instantly. Our families grew, and we spent almost every day together. We learned how to be mommas while figuring out the whole discipline thing with toddlers together. Oh, the stories we can tell!

She was the one friend that I was literally heart-broken over when we relocated halfway across the US in 1999. She was the first friend (other than my husband) that I was able to connect with about my faith... or lack thereof. Further along in her spiritual life, she had been a beacon for me. We had spent lots of time talking about how to be a good wife, parent... you name it, we talked about it!

Sitting at her kitchen table, catching up on our grown adult children scattered across the country, and reminiscing about old times, was pure balm to my soul. Acknowledging our mistakes was insightful. Looking back at how we parented and did life 25+ years ago was quite eye-opening. I'd like to think we have grown in wisdom!

We talked about how in the first phase of our lives we were busy figuring it out, learning and soaking up everything we could about "how" to do life in a God-honoring way-- asking God to intervene and help. And now, in the second phase of our lives, we must take time to sit in silence and contemplate things. Literally, spend time...not talking TO God...but LISTENING to what he has to say to us. After 25 years of always talking TO God, it's very hard to flip the switch and be still, to just listen, to meditate on a Scripture and ask God to reveal himself. But it is key to making this phase meaningful.

We are brainwashed in today's world that we must be constantly busy. Most are fearful that others will think we are lazy if we choose to say, "NO" to yet another thing. That we aren't doing enough. That we are not offering the best to our children. That we are not providing quality time, activities, options for our family. But God wants us to seek him, and steer our families towards him. That may mean scheduling time differently than others.

How are you doing being still and listening to God? Make it a priority and you'll be blessed!

My soul,
wait in silence
for God alone,
for my hope
is from Him.
-Psalm 62:5

Do something about it: *When can you schedule time, away from all distractions, to be still and listen to what God has to say to you?*

_____

_____

_____

NOW'S THE TIME

Beth Frank loves Jesus, her hubs, her three girls, and thinking creatively. Beth is the co-founder of KidzMatter. She also owns a design company called B Frank Design Co. She was inspired by her oldest daughter's autism diagnosis to write the book Ausomely Blessed.

Ever feel like you just aren't enough for the job? That your skills don't match up to the requirements? Maybe you don't feel that you communicate influentially and that you lack eloquence.

Can you imagine being asked to go back to a country where you were wanted for murder and speak to the most powerful man in the known world and tell him to release a million or so slaves that did critical work for him in the name of a God that this king had no respect for? No small task at all! Moses wasn't sure he was up for this, but God knew He had assigned this monumental task to the right person. Exodus 3:11 and 4:10 record Moses' objections that he is unworthy of the job and begs to be excused, but God promises his presence and guidance.

When millions of lives were on the line, God came through for Moses again and again.

Somewhere along the way, between parting the Red Sea and the Ten Commandments, Moses emerges as one of the greatest leaders recorded in Scripture.

Maybe you feel secure in your leadership capabilities, but now just doesn't seem like the time that you should step up to one more deadline, obligation or challenge. The responsibility and load of leading an effective children's ministry could mean the death of the nice, quiet, orderly life you currently live.

Queen Esther felt the same way, only her circumstances were much more dire. She was facing a possible death sentence by coming before the king without being summoned and a certain death sentence for being a Jew. Her uncle, Mordecai, doesn't give her an "easy out". Esther 4:14 records Mordecai's response to his niece, you are here "for such a time as this". There has never been a more pivotal time to jump in with both feet into what God is calling you to do. For such a time as this you have been called, don't hesitate!

Have you jumped into leadership whole-heartedly, invested in others and trusted in God for the outcome, but you just don't feel that anyone is following? In II Peter 2:15 Noah is described as a "preacher of righteousness". Noah obeyed God and built an ark, but Scripture is clear that no one besides Noah and his immediate family boarded the ark to safety. I'm sure that the wickedness and lack of belief were discouraging to Noah as he day after day continued his work on the ark.

Don't lose heart, God has given you specific plans to carry out. Day after day, work for Him and follow His blueprint for your ministry. As you continue to "preach righteousness," He alone will bring about the outcome.

These Biblical figures are all ordinary people, but serving an extraordinary God. Let them serve as an example to us all. God supplies the strength, courage, grace, conviction, boldness, and passion that we need for leadership. If he calls you, he most certainly will equip you. Go lead your ministry with the confidence that the One you serve goes before you and with you!

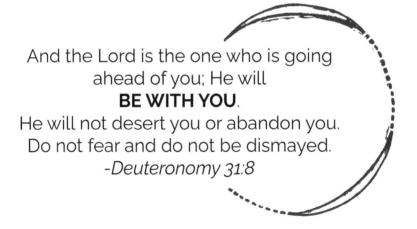

And the Lord is the one who is going ahead of you; He will
BE WITH YOU.
He will not desert you or abandon you.
Do not fear and do not be dismayed.
-Deuteronomy 31:8

Pray about it: *Ask God to show you where he wants you to right now step up and lead. What areas have you had a tender heart or an urgency in your soul to help. Ask God to give you divine wisdom and strength to jump in and lead for such a time as this.*

_____

_____

_____

INCREASING AND DECREASING

Joshua Cooley is a longtime kids ministry leader and a New York Times bestselling author whose many books include kids and youth devotionals. www.joshuacooleyauthor.com

Can you imagine what it must have been like to be John the Baptist?

- When choosing his habitat, he went full-bore Bear Grylls, opting for the wilderness.
- He had a curious choice of clothing, favoring an itchy camel-hair garment (quite unlike the posh camel-hair coats you'll find today at Saks Fifth Avenue).
- He did not have a discerning palate. Of course, desert dining options are fairly limited. It was either his well-known honey-dipped locusts or perhaps "scorpion surprise." Mmmm!
- When he saw the religious leaders approaching, he shouted, "You offspring of vipers, who warned you to flee from the wrath to come?" Born prophet? Yes. Public relations director? Not so much.

John certainly was quite a guy. As the last of the Old Testament prophets, he was charged with directly introducing God's long-awaited Messiah (Matthew 11:10). Jesus himself praised John by saying, *"Among those born of women, there has not arisen anyone greater than John the Baptist"* (Matthew 11:11).

In his brief public ministry, John was also wildly popular. As he preached repentance and baptized in the Jordan River, Jews from Jerusalem and all over Judea flocked to him, wondering if he was the Anointed One.

John could've reveled in his renown. He could've become like King Saul or Absalom, who tasted power and influence and liked it too much. Instead, when Jesus arrived at the Jordan, John deflected the spotlight and exclaimed, *"Behold, the Lamb of God who takes away the sin of the world!"* (John 1:29). Shortly afterward, John fully deferred his ministry to Christ, saying, *"He must increase, but I must decrease"* (John 3:30).

As a kid's ministry leader, you have been afforded a position of some authority and influence. Perhaps fame even occasionally shines upon you (e.g. speaking engagements, writing opportunities, etc.). Modern-day kid's ministry, in its own strange ways, can quickly foster cults of personality in churches of all sizes. If we're not careful, the focus can shift to the individuals running the program—or the details of the program itself—instead of the Savior who rules over all.

Kid's ministry should always be about Christ and his gospel, not about us. Like John, use your influence to deflect the spotlight to the Messiah as you let John's mantra become yours:

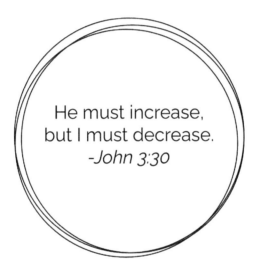

He must increase,
but I must decrease.
-John 3:30

Think about it: *Is the gospel proclaimed each week in your classrooms? Are there parts of your ministry where Jesus needs to increase?*

_____

_____

_____

_____

_____

_____

TEAM JESUS

Beth Frank loves Jesus, her hubs, her three girls, and thinking creatively. Beth is the co-founder of KidzMatter. She also owns a design company called B Frank Design Co. She was inspired by her oldest daughter's autism diagnosis to write the book Ausomely Blessed.

"I don't work for man's applause. I don't work for man's applause. I don't work for man's applause."

How many times have I replayed that mantra in my mind? I do this while trying not to indulge in disappointment and a mini "pity me" party because I didn't hear the praise and affirming words I so longed to hear after a job well done?

As leaders in kidmin, we are in a unique sandwich position—sandwiched between the expectations of church leadership and the expectations of parents. Sometimes these expectations can be miles apart and the affirming words we long to hear from both sides never cross those miles. How can we as leaders remain steadfast in sometimes thankless situations?

The key is knowing whose team you're on. When I'm rooting for and trying to bring glory to Team Beth, I'm going to be disappointed every time! I need to daily "do life" on Team Jesus. He alone uniquely calls, divinely equips, and amazingly empowers us to service!

Every believer has a unique calling. It's true! Sometimes though I just want to quit. I don't think I'm the only one that feels this way. I want to walk away from ministry, and sometimes the people in ministry, and never return. (Hopefully, no one in my church is reading this devotional book. Yikes, this is real honesty here! #graceplease). When this happens it's because I've got a focus problem. I'm not focusing on Jesus and His unique purpose for me. When I focus on Him and his calling for my life, I realize I never want to quit serving Him. And seriously, those of us called to kidmin know we have the best calling there is. We can't quit! #TeamJesusForever

Ephesians 2:10 says, *"For we are his workmanship, created in Christ Jesus for good works, which God prepared beforehand, that we should walk in them."* Living life without human thanks is difficult, but we have been divinely equipped to handle the ministry God has uniquely called us to. We can do more than just "handle" our current ministry placement; we can prosper because He has made and developed us with all the tools for the trade that we need! From leading a first grader in a salvation prayer, to dealing with a defiant tween to respecting a leadership team that doesn't seem to be supportive of our role—and everything else in between—He gives and grows us to be up to the challenge.

#TeamJesusReady

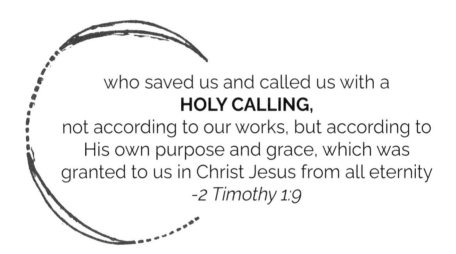

who saved us and called us with a
HOLY CALLING,
not according to our works, but according to His own purpose and grace, which was granted to us in Christ Jesus from all eternity
-2 Timothy 1:9

Pray about it: Stop, tune in and listen. If you do, you will hear the sound of the voice of your loudest cheerleader. No one loves you more, wants your ministry to succeed more, cares more, knows more, understands more, hurts with you more, and is eternally invested more than Jesus. He is your loudest cheerleader. Stop and listen for HIS voice above the rest, because His is the only one which matters! #TeamJesusStrong

_____

_____

_____

_____

SHUT OUT NEGATIVE VOICES

Ryan Frank is a pastor, publisher, and entrepreneur. He serves as CEO of KidzMatter, co-founder of KidzMatter Mega-Con, and CEO of Frank Insurance Agency. Ryan and his wife, Beth, run several businesses and love to travel and spend time with their three daughters.
ryanfrank.com

I've been working with leaders for many years now. Here's what I have found. Most people know what they need to do, and they know exactly the right thing to get them where they need to be, but the roadblock, the obstacle that gets them every time is this: they are listening to the wrong voices.

They can have the map laid out right in front of them and know exactly where it is they need to go, but too many people listen to the wrong voices, and they end up stopping short of where they need to go.

What voices are you listening to?

We put way too much emphasis and importance on the voices of those around us that shouldn't have that voice. They shouldn't have that influence in our life. There are people around you (it should be a small group) that you want and that you need speaking into your life and into your future.

More often than not you get into trouble because you are listening to the wrong voices, those voices that say, "you can't." The voices of those that say you are going to fail, there's no way you are going to make it, there's no way you can launch that, or there's no way you can become that.

Sometimes those voices are voices of actual real people. They are those negative people around us. Most of the time the people who boo loudest in the stands are those that never had the courage to go out on the field in the beginning. And here you are. You're out in the field listening to those in the stands telling you that you can't do it. They are not the ones that you should be listening to.

Sometimes those voices come from inside of us. Those voices of fear that say, "What if I fail?" Those voices of insecurity that say, "I don't know if I have what it takes." Those voices of past regrets that say, "What if I do that again?" Those voices of past hurts that say, "Don't do that. It's only going to cost you. It cost you before, and it will cost you again."

Learn to listen to the right voices in your life. Shut out the voices of those that are negative. Shut out the voices of those that tell you that you can't do it. Those voices that come from inside of you that say you can't do this, you don't measure up, or you can't get this done! Instead, listen to the voice of truth.

Do you remember that old Casting Crowns song, "The Voice of Truth"? Start listening to the voice of truth as found in God's Word.

You are who God says you are. You can do what His Holy Spirit empowers you to do. You can be what He wants you and purposes for you to be.

When you begin to listen to those voices of truth, that is going to be a game changer for you! You are going to grow your confidence. You are going to all of a sudden believe that you can do this. You are not only going to grow in your confidence, but you will have the courage and the determination to take those steps you need to take and have the courage to get from where you are today to where you know you need to be. But it is going to require listening to the voice of truth!

But blessed is the one who
TRUSTS IN THE LORD,
whose confidence is in him.
-*Jeremiah 17:7*

Pray about it: *Shut out those negative voices. Spend some time, right now, listening to the Voice of Truth. What is he telling you?*

_____

_____

_____

THE LORD'S SERVANT

Jaye Lynne Rooney is the co-director of Children's Ministry at Asbury United Methodist Church in Pasadena, TX (East Houston). She loves getting to be a part of kids' first introductions to faith and the God who they will come to know as their very best friend.

Have you ever sat at your desk and thought, "I am a failure"? Perhaps your event had few attendees. Maybe kids aren't enjoying Sunday School. Or you could simply be out of ideas and exhausted. Whatever the cause, you feel like a failure and are certain you are letting people down.

You could say that Mary was given the most challenging children's ministry job ever. She was called to raise the Son of God. She must have felt so ill-equipped. Mary had no training or degrees. She didn't have reference books or Facebook groups. She didn't even have kids already. Yet from the very beginning she recognized that God's sovereignty meant that she was capable of living up to her calling.

"I am the Lord's servant," was Mary's reply to the angel.

This should be your response, too, when God calls you to do his work. I am the Lord's servant. The only person who could be a failure is the person who is in charge - and the good news for those in ministry is that you are not that person. God is the master. He alone can be judged as a failure or a success. (Spoiler alert: he's a success.) Everyone working in the ministry are servants only. What a relief!

The feeling of being a failure is actually a deceitful trick. It turns your eyes from God to yourself and you begin to rely on your own abilities. But as servants you are responsible only for following God's will. As Mary also said, God knew her "humble state" when he chose her. She was certain he would equip her for the task. And this is the wonderful truth for all of His disciples. God doesn't call you to fail. He will equip you, no matter the task. You just need to respond "Yes, I am the Lord's servant!"

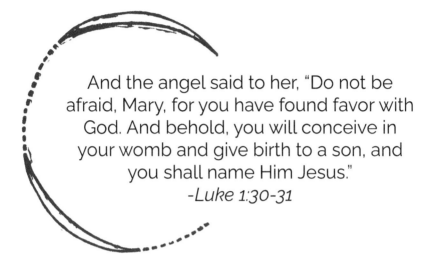

And the angel said to her, "Do not be afraid, Mary, for you have found favor with God. And behold, you will conceive in your womb and give birth to a son, and you shall name Him Jesus."
-Luke 1:30-31

Do something about it: *Begin giving your to-do list this week a new heading, like "I am God's Servant" or "I Serve Like Mary."*

_____

_____

_____

DRAWING A CHILD'S HEART CLOSE TO GOD

__Beth Frank__ loves Jesus, her hubs, her three girls, and thinking creatively. Beth is the co-founder of KidzMatter. She also owns a design company called B Frank Design Co. She was inspired by her oldest daughter's autism diagnosis to write the book Ausomely Blessed.

Our biggest responsibility (and probably greatest challenge) as parents and kidmin leaders is drawing a child's heart close to God. In my own household with three girls ages sixteen, eleven, and seven, it seems that every day, in their own way, they draw my heart close to God with their innocence and child-like faith. My most powerful God-encounters have all involved my girls. Prayerfully, I'm not the only beneficiary of our relationship. I pray that they are drawn closer to God through interacting with me. Every day, my job is to provide opportunities for my little ladies (this Momma likes to refer to them as ladies hoping the title will rub off) to know, love, and serve Jesus more.

The Know Part: I'm not just talking about head knowledge here. While it's important that our kiddos know the Bible and be able to defend their faith, a heart knowledge is so much more critical. Are we modeling Christ-like behavior in a way that makes those that follow us want to know Jesus?

I recently had a conversation with a 15-year-old boy at church who got into trouble because of some misbehavior. The statements he made about his life and those in his life broke my heart. What he faces on a daily basis I can't even begin to fathom. I left that conversation thinking how much more of a challenge it was for this boy to know Jesus and understand his love because of the circumstances he had already lived through at such young age.

Proverbs 4:23 says *"Watch over your heart with all diligence, For from it flow the springs of life."* Let's do our part to protect the little people we have been entrusted with by giving them a clear path to knowing Jesus.

The Love Part: If you are a kidmin leader, then chances are you are already gifted in this area. You love kids and kids love you!!! This is what brings you back every week.

I can't think of any earthly person who showed me more love growing up than my grandpa. It wasn't a coincidence that he taught me more about the love of Jesus than anyone else. Nothing will draw children (and parents for that matter) closer to Jesus than unconditional love.

The Serve Part: Once our little ones know Jesus, they easily will fall in love with him and the natural outcome of loving him is to serve him. How exciting to be charged with providing these little world changers with opportunities to do just that.

I have a sign hanging in my oldest daughter's room that says, "Someday I'm going to change the world." I chose the sign because the colors match her room perfectly, but I don't really agree with what it says. Luci Frank is changing her world today, not "someday."

Do the kids in your ministry know that they can make a significant difference in their world today?

And now, Israel, what does the Lord your God require of you, but to fear the Lord your God, to walk in all His ways and love Him, and to serve the Lord your God with all your heart and with all 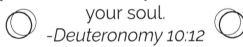 your soul.
-Deuteronomy 10:12

Pray about it: What does "know, love, and serve" mean to you? Here's a challenge. Pick one thing you can do in each of these areas beginning this Sunday. Then pray that God will take your efforts and use them for His glory.

_____

_____

_____

_____

_____

I WANT IT NOW!

Corinne Noble is a children's pastor, curriculum creator, and author. She enjoys writing curriculum, creating set designs, and sharing her ideas with other kidmin leaders at kmccurriculum.com.

I'm really impatient. There, I said it. I tell people all the time that I struggle with being patient. Impatience can become a huge hinderance in following God. I believe we are all becoming more and more impatient because of the culture we live in. Our culture is an instant gratification culture. We don't just want coffee, we want it now! Starbucks came out with a feature on their app that allows us to order ahead of time, skip the wait, grab our coffee, and go! That's just one example of culture feeding into the "I want it now" mentality. We can get music, money, food, and just about any product instantly or within a few hours.

Not everything in life works that way, especially when it comes to ministry. Think about it. What do you want right now for your ministry that you just can't seem to attain? Is it resources, money, space, time, volunteers, paid staff... your own sanity? If I had to guess, we all want one or more of those things for our ministries. Why can't we have it right now? It would just be so much easier, right? Of course, that's how it feels to us, but God has something different in mind for us and our ministries. So, how do we overcome the "I want it now" attitude that is so deeply engrained in our minds and in our culture?

1. Wait patiently. Ok, I might still be stuck on step 1. Those two words sound so simple, but they are so hard to put into practice. I have to constantly remind myself to be patient and wait. The struggle is real (at least for me)! I love what Romans 8:25 says: *"But if we hope for what we do not see, through perseverance we wait eagerly for it."*

2. Trust in God's timing. God's timing is usually not the same as ours. This is the main reason we can't have what we want, when we want it. God has reasons behind why he is making us wait. We may not see those reasons now (or ever), but we must rest assured that God is always at work behind the scenes. Ecclesiastes 3:11 tells us, *"He has made everything appropriate in its time. He has also set eternity in their heart, without the possibility that mankind will find out the work which God has done from the beginning even to the end."*

3. Ask, "What is God teaching me?" This is an important step. We may be in a season of waiting because God is trying to teach us something new. I believe that God is trying to teach me to rely on his strength and power right now, rather than on my own abilities and talents. I like to believe that I can fix any situation if I just work hard enough. I can brainstorm and worry myself to death over a situation, and then realize I never prayed about it. God wants us to bring our needs and concerns to him first, not after we have tried everything we can think of to fix it ourselves. What is God trying to teach you while you wait?

4. Listen to his voice. I find that it is hard to hear God's voice when I am constantly busy talking and working. Sometimes we just need to be still and listen to God. I definitely struggle with stopping and being quiet. I'm certain there have been many times when I have missed something God was trying to tell me because I wasn't listening. James 1:19 says, *"Now everyone must be quick to hear, slow to speak, and slow to anger;"*

If you aren't spending time being still and quiet before the Lord, start today. Start small and take five minutes each day to just listen to God.

5. Follow his plan. Notice the key word in that sentence is "his". We love making our own plans. Anyone else love to-do lists as much as I do? Just like our timing is often not the same as God's timing, our plans are also a bit different. If we aren't intentional about doing the first four steps, we probably aren't following God's plan. When we follow our own plan, we miss out on a bigger and greater plan that God has for us. Proverbs 3:5-6 is still one of my favorite passages in the Bible. *"Trust in the Lord with all your heart and do not lean on your own understanding. In all your ways acknowledge him, and he will make your paths straight."* We don't need to depend on our own ideas and plans. If we just turn to God, he will show us the steps we need to take."

Make room for still moments for him to speak to you. When it's time to move, make sure you are following his plan instead of your own.

> But if we hope for what we do not see, through
> perseverance we wait eagerly for it.
> *-Romans 8:25*

Think about it: *What is God asking you to wait for? Trust in his timing. Ask him to reveal what you need to learn from the experience.*

_____

_____

REMEMBER AND KNOW

Amber Pike is the editor of KidzMatter Magazine, an author, a children's minister, and a momma whose passion is to see kids loving the Word of God and walking with Him!
www.amberpike.org

One of the most important lessons I learned about kidmin (before God even called me into it) is to remember a child's name. Serving in VBS at 15 years old, finally old enough to be a co-teacher instead of just a helper, I heard the teacher over and over again call kids by the wrong name. They hated it. I could see it in their little 3-year-old eyes. They didn't feel known. They didn't feel loved, and they wanted to.

Kids want to be called by the right name. They crave it. Knowing and using a child's name communicates the value you place on them. The simple act of remembering their name tells them that they are important to you, and that they are important to Jesus.

Whether names come easily to you or not, knowing a child's name is important. I make it my personal goal to know every child's name. Even visitors. If you've been to my church at least twice, I should know your name! (Only the kids though... I'm not so good with knowing the adult's names!)

Know their name! Use their names! But... you can do better.

Yes, you have to know their names (and allergy information and what class they are in), but what else do you know about the children in your ministry? How well do you know each child? Do you know what sports they play, who their friends are at school, or what their favorite candy is? Believe it or not, those things matter, because each and every child matters. They matter to Jesus, so they need to matter to you. God has entrusted these boys and girls in your care to shepherd and lead, but also to love.

Love on them with the love of Jesus. KNOW them. Remember their name, and each time that you do, give thanks for that precious blessing.

I thank my God
in all my remembrance
of you.
-*Philippians 1:3*

Do something about it: *Do a quick check. How much can you remember about each child in your ministry? What can do you to show the kids that they are known and loved by you this week?*

_____

_____

_____

_____

_____

_____

TAKE HEART

Beth Frank *loves Jesus, her hubs, her three girls, and thinking creatively. Beth is the co-founder of KidzMatter. She also owns a design company called B Frank Design Co. She was inspired by her oldest daughter's autism diagnosis to write the book Ausomely Blessed.*

Recently this verse was our daughter Londyn's Awana verse for the week. *"These things I have spoken to you so that in Me you may have peace. In the world you have tribulation, but take courage; I have overcome the world,"* John 16:33. I have always found encouragement in this reference, but that particular week it was what my heart needed so much. I love how God coordinates the details of our lives and he had assigned this verse to Londyn the very week that I needed to hear it, the very week that the Bible study I was teaching covered a topic that this verse speaks to. As I found myself repeating it over and over in my mind during the week and as Londyn practiced reciting it to me, I had time to ponder and again be reminded of the foundational truths in this verse.

It's not a shocking statement that life is hard, and that ministry life sometimes can be even harder. All of us in kidmin stand on the front lines of battle week after week waging war for the children and families in our communities. It can become overwhelming, it can be discouraging, it can seem like a losing battle. According to John 16:33 this should not surprise us. Tribulation is promised, it's not "if" it's coming, but "when". Jesus reminds us though that He is offering peace, not a peace without strife or adversity, but a peace that co-exists with conflict and struggle. One thing that I hadn't noticed before but realized as I have studied this verse more fully is that the tribulation is promised, but peace isn't. Peace is offered, but not promised. Jesus is speaking these things to us so that we will seek his way and not let the world come between us and him so that we will have the peace he is offering to us.

My ministry friend, if the world has overcome you by coming between you and your relationship with the one who offers peace, take heart, because he has overcome the world! The timing of this verse cannot be ignored. When he spoke these words, Jesus was coming to the end of his earthly ministry and would soon be facing the cross. Even as he speaks these words, things are happening that are putting into motion Christ's death on the cross. Yet, he speaks of peace, he has peace in his circumstances and also has enough to give to others.

Even the shadow of the cross cannot take away from the victory that is certain. If you are in a season of tribulation, this isn't a pep talk meant to help you "cheer up" or tell you to strive more, but a gentle reminder that victory has already been secured. His victory secures ours!

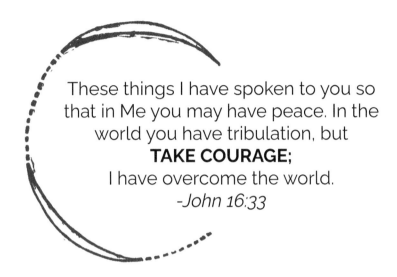

These things I have spoken to you so that in Me you may have peace. In the world you have tribulation, but
TAKE COURAGE;
I have overcome the world.
-John 16:33

Do something about it: *Take heart kidmin family, pray, and then keep bravely taking the next step forward, willingly accepting the peace our Savior offers! Victory is yours!!*

_____

_____

_____

SOW THOSE SEEDS?

Vanessa Myers is a children's minister, author, and blogger who loves to create resources for families to help them grow in their faith together.
www.vanessamyers.org

Several years ago, I came across a letter that my grandmother (Mema) wrote to me one summer while I was working at church camp during my college years. Here's what she wrote:

> Dear Vanessa,
>
> I hear you are enjoying your work as a counselor and I am sure you are a good guide to those children. Your smile and your attitude toward life is certainly inspiring. You will never know probably how much you have helped those children.
>
> Love,
>
> Mema

One sentence from this letter has really stuck with me as I think about my life as a children's pastor: "You will never know probably how much you have helped those children." Isn't that the truth! I never know what kind of impact I am making in the life of a child. Are they listening to me? Do they even understand what I am saying? Do they really believe in Jesus? Is what I am teaching and doing making an impact and helping them grow in their faith?

As a children's pastor, I am a seed planter. I plant seeds of faith into the lives of children. I pray the children I work with will walk with the Lord all the days of their lives. I pray they will always know that Jesus loves them no matter what. I pray they will seek him and praise him, even in the most difficult times.

My grandmother was right... I may never truly know the impact I make on a child's life. However, I pray maybe one day I will see the seeds I planted bloom in their lives. I pray I might be able to catch a glimpse of these children doing great things for the Lord. Maybe I will and maybe I won't, but that does not stop me from continuing to do the work of the Lord and planting those seeds of faith into all children. I pray you will see the importance of your role in a child's life. Keep planting those seeds, because as the verse below says, God will "multiply your seed for sowing and increase the harvest of your righteousness."

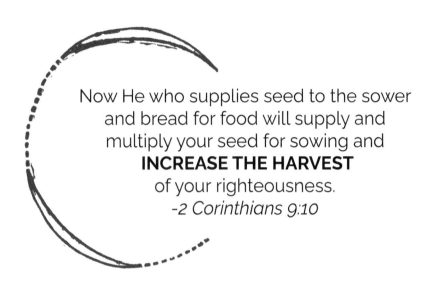

Now He who supplies seed to the sower
and bread for food will supply and
multiply your seed for sowing and
INCREASE THE HARVEST
of your righteousness.
-2 Corinthians 9:10

Think about it: *What are you doing to plant seeds of faith into the lives of children? What else can you do to help children know Jesus more?*

_____

_____

_____

_____

_____

_____

GOD APPOINTMENTS

***Beth Frank** loves Jesus, her hubs, her three girls, and thinking creatively. Beth is the co-founder of KidzMatter. She also owns a design company called B Frank Design Co. She was inspired by her oldest daughter's autism diagnosis to write the book Ausomely Blessed.*

As children and family pastors we have the unique opportunity to look at life and ministry through the lens of the next generation. This should be shaping more than our thoughts and ideas. It should also be shaping the basic way we live. If I am actively using my brief time on this earth doing kingdom building in such a way that it touches future generations, I need to be intentional and sacrificial.

I think we all agree that we want to make a lasting difference, but sometimes it's a discouraging task because we think what is required is too great, or takes a lifetime of service, or requires having a large platform of influence that reaches the masses. Yes, it's true that any one of those things on their own can make a lasting impact, but they aren't required. What's required is sacrifice. Rarely will something of great value take place without significant personal sacrifice.

Intentionality with sacrifice can bridge the gap between the magnitude of the call, lack of time, and the size of your ministry. Don't ever be intimidated by the magnitude of next generation ministry.

It does sound intimidating when words like, sacrifice, intentionality, actively, shaping, and significant are thrown around. The idea that I have something to share and pass on to another generation that will make a difference in years to come is overwhelming and intimidating to be sure. That's ok, because we aren't called to do it alone. God, working through us as we sacrificially serve, is who makes the impact.

So today, take a deep breath and release all of those overwhelming and unrealistic expectations you have placed on yourself. You don't have to carry that burden. Christ, in you, will make the difference!

Our God can take a brief moment of sacrificial service and multiply that influence in a student's life exponentially. How many times have you been in a moment that you didn't even see coming, but the hair on your neck stands straight up because you know that you are in a "God appointment". Pray for God to give you these assignments and be open to His leading. The magnitude of what God is able to accomplish in these moments will not be known this side of heaven. We don't need the entire elementary years of a child's life to influence their future. For many of us, having a child that faithfully attends our ministry during that time span isn't even a reality. You might only have one Sunday with a lot of kids, but it's still possible to make a lifetime impact.

Sacrifice for the next generation calls us to actively serve those around us that God has placed into our lives. Make the sacrifice to choose God's plans today and give yourself completely to those plans. Be ready and present to the "God appointments" that are scheduled for you today!! The generations that follow you will be so grateful and blessed that you did!!

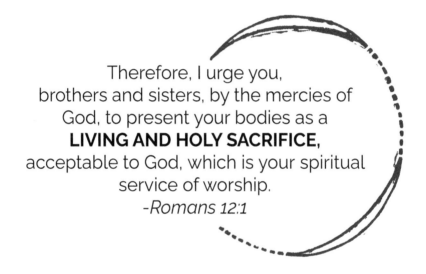

Therefore, I urge you,
brothers and sisters, by the mercies of
God, to present your bodies as a
LIVING AND HOLY SACRIFICE,
acceptable to God, which is your spiritual
service of worship.
-Romans 12:1

Pray about it: *Pray daily to have the eyes, ears, and heart of Jesus. Ask to be shown someone that needs love today. These are the assignments that God has for us that will make lasting impacts. You don't need a microphone, blog, website, or large vibrant ministry to touch one soul today, just an open heart and willingness to follow the Spirit's leading.*

_____

_____

_____

_____

POLICY AND PROCEDURE PHOBIA

__Beth Frank__ loves Jesus, her hubs, her three girls, and thinking creatively. Beth is the co-founder of KidzMatter. She also owns a design company called B Frank Design Co. She was inspired by her oldest daughter's autism diagnosis to write the book Ausomely Blessed.

It's confession time... I have a real aversion to anything related to policy, procedures, or time management. This area is definitely not one of my strengths and I definitely prefer to be creative and not be committed or nailed down to any certain plan. Recently though, the Lord has brought me back to one of my very favorite books of the Bible, Philippians. I read verses that I have read and heard many times throughout my life, but this time it jumped off the page and I have been meditating on it ever since.

These verses have given me a renewed passion to see my identity in Christ and not in possessions, the opinion of others, or my success or failures; or how well I do with policies, procedures and time management. For sure this is a work in progress and is a daily battle for me to keep my focus eternal and not temporal. My future is Jesus! Beyond that, everything else is peripheral. I encourage you that you would remember that policies and procedures are great, important and needed, but they are not your identity as a kidmin leader.

In ministry it's often difficult to separate our identity from how well our programs run, the size of our ministry, and the policies and procedures that we've created to run those ministries. The line between personal significance and significant kingdom building is sometimes blurred when we lose track of our identity in Christ.

If you've lost the joy, freedom, and creativity in your personal calling, it might not be burnout, it could be an identity crisis. Without intentional focus, our identity can shift and become tied up in the opinions of others (like the pastors we serve under or the families we serve), or in comparing our ministry to others, or looking at the impact we've made with our families or in our communities. There is nothing wrong with regularly evaluating how we are doing in our current area of service, but our identity and significance cannot come from our title or achievements.

Our identity is found in Christ alone, everything else is loss.

But whatever things were gain to me, these things
I have counted as loss because of Christ. More
than that, I count all things to be loss in view of
the surpassing value of knowing Christ Jesus
my Lord, for whom I have suffered the loss of all
things, and count them mere rubbish, so that I may
gain Christ, and may be found in Him, not having a
righteousness of my own derived from the Law,
but that which is through faith in Christ, the
righteousness which comes from God on the basis
of faith, that I may know Him and the power of His
resurrection and the fellowship of His sufferings,
being conformed to His death;
-Philippians 3:7-10

Pray about it: *Ask God to help you see yourself the way He does and that the truth of scripture would be where you find your identity and worth.*

_____

_____

_____

_____

_____

_____

THE DEVIL DOESN'T TAKE A DAY OFF. BUT YOU SHOULD

Sam Beam is a preteen pastor and host of the Navigating Preteen Ministry Podcast. A Georgia native and recently married he enjoys camping, computers, and cooking.

"The Devil doesn't take a day off." This is a phrase we hear often, especially in ministry. Oftentimes it's a justification for the long hours, hard work, and late nights put into the church.

My question is... how long have we modeled after the Devil?

So often the church is full of great intentioned, hard-working, and fiercely loyal pastors, but what happened to rest? Burnout is an ever-looming fear, not to mention the forgotten family, friends, and passions you once had. If you're not careful, ministry can consume every aspect of your life.

If you have spent any time in ministry, you have seen it happen to friends, fellow pastors, or co-workers. Ministry becomes too much and we simply drop out.

What's the solution? How can we overcome the pressures of the Ministry? I want to propose a not-so-new idea: Sabbath.

The Bible is clear, a Sabbath rest is needed. If God can rest, so can you. Rest comes in many forms, from a walk in nature to an amazing home-cooked meal. The point is we need to take time to rest. Pick a day where you can unplug, turn off your phone, and rest. If you have a family, spend time with your kids, your spouse, and the Lord. Read a great book, eat good food, and enjoy resting in the world God gave us all.

Now that might sound easy, but implementation can be hard. Setting aside a whole day to not work is a commitment and if you're not intentional with it, it simply won't happen. So, here's the challenge: find your community and rally together. Set a day of the week, or even start with a half-day and unplug. Turn your phone off, place your full attention to what is in front of you, and rest. Sleep in, meditate on God's Word, connect with loved ones, and recharge.

Sabbath rest is not a scary thing, or even a boring one. Sabbath in its fullest form is a time where we follow God's example and step back, observe what we have, and recharge for the week ahead. So, rest. Don't ignore a command that's been in place for a millennia and take steps against the world's ever eroding presence.

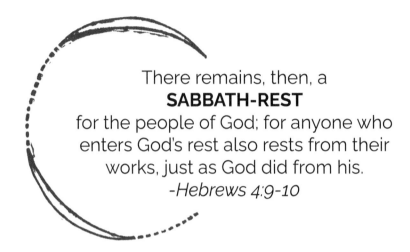

There remains, then, a
SABBATH-REST
for the people of God; for anyone who enters God's rest also rests from their works, just as God did from his.
-Hebrews 4:9-10

Do something about it: *Take time to rest. Plan a Sabbath day (or half-day or even a few hours) this week and rest. Spend time with the Father and rest in him.*

_____

_____

_____

EXHAUSTED
BUT STILL IN PURSUIT!

Jack Henry is a veteran Family Pastor and has served at various churches over the past 38 years. He is more compassionate now than ever and still longs to be used by God to produce Kingdom growth. You can reach him at oldkidspastor@gmail.com

We ALL can identify with the account of Gideon and his men from Judges 8:4. What powerful words they are, especially that word... EXHAUSTED.

> *Then Gideon and the three hundred men who were with him came to the Jordan and crossed over, exhausted yet still pursuing.*

Ministry can be and will always be exhausting. Believe me when I say that there is no way around it because I have looked for a "way" for almost 40 years! But why? Why is ministry exhausting? Let me list a few reasons:

1. Because we are dealing with people. People who have the same problems that we have and at times, worse. Until we die or Jesus returns, this will be the case. People are needy. Jesus said that we are all like "sheep." Oh boy! We have been identified with the dumbest and most needy animal on the planet.

2. Because sin is real. People get caught up into all kinds of crazy stuff. Bad decisions are made. Families are torn apart. The list is huge. We all know that Satan is working without ceasing to tear down and destroy.

3. Because we are in a battle. It is a spiritual battle but nonetheless, it's real! This battle can be draining on us at times, and it gets very hard to stand and fight; especially when we have families of our own and all the responsibilities that come with it.

4. Because most of you are not full-time in ministry. Praise God for you! If not for you, then most children's ministries would have no one! With all of your personal family responsibilities, you also carry the burdens of many that lean on you and depend on you for comfort and direction.

This is why we need God more than ever! This is why we need to be filled, daily, with his Holy Spirit! We cannot do this in our own strength.

Many of you have tried and you know what the outcome was. BURNOUT.

But another word listed in this verse gives the very reason why we keep going… "PURSUIT!"

What was Gideon and his 300 men in pursuit of? The enemy! Even though Gideon requested food and drink to be provided for his men (Judges 8:5-7) and supplies were denied them, they kept going. It is so important to surround yourself with a team of people that have the same passion and vision as you do.

No doubt Gideon loved and cared for these 300 men. No doubt he wanted the best for them and offered them great encouragement. The fact remains that these men were in it to win it! That's the kind of people we need on our team! Do what you have to do to make that happen.

The pursuit will not end until Jesus returns, so let's stay faithful. Jesus is coming and his reward for us as well!

Then Gideon and the three hundred men who were with him came to the Jordan and crossed over, exhausted yet still pursuing.
-Judges 8:4

Think about it: *What kind of team have you surrounded yourself with? Are you leading (or contributing) your team with encouragement, even when they are exhausted?*

_____

_____

_____

CHURCH, LOVE, AND GEN Z

Beth Frank loves Jesus, her hubs, her three girls, and thinking creatively. Beth is the co-founder of KidzMatter. She also owns a design company called B Frank Design Co. She was inspired by her oldest daughter's autism diagnosis to write the book Ausomely Blessed.

Most of the kids that we minster to today are a part of the generation that is sometimes referred to as Generation Z. I'm not sure of the origin of that name, but it seems appropriate to me because the challenges that these kids face run the gamut from A to Z. Many kids today in our North American culture face things that I myself can't even wrap my brain around.

I recently met a girl at church who lived with her Mom and Grandma. She told me that she was sad because her second brother was just sent to prison and her Grandma was facing cancer. Increasingly we are ministering to a generation that is being raised in the reality of difficult family dynamics, substance abuse, materialism, poverty, violence in school, educational disparity, and a shifting economy. The hard reality is that kids have to grow up way too fast.

What does that mean for the church today? Much in our cultural, societal, political, and educational landscape has changed from a generation ago, but has the church changed to be a more effective light to this new generation? We can't expect to "do church" within our four safe walls - the way we always have - and get results. In some churches programming has become sacred and we can't change anything because that would be downright "blasphemy."

Traditionally, kids come to church and sit in teacher-led classes to learn about God and his love for them. If a child comes and doesn't quite fit in because they can't attend regularly, or sitting still for that long is impossible, or they have never been to church before and "church culture" is as foreign to them as visiting China, what do we do with these kids?

Now more than ever we have an influx of children that just don't fit the mold of our traditional programs. We have amazing programs, but do we have amazing results? To reach this new generation, we must think beyond the four walls of our church building and our perfectly planned programs. This is a huge challenge. While I don't have a perfect solution, I know something that can make a huge difference -- Love!

This sounds simple and trite, but if we let love lead us out of the traditional and into the new, greater things can be accomplished. When radical love for Jesus and the children in our ministry is our priority over programming and perfectly set up classrooms, then real, radical things will happen. Love will take us beyond the safe, beyond our scheduled ministry times, beyond the status quo and will open new venues for service and relationships that will affect this generation like nothing else.

And have
MERCY
on some,
who are doubting
-Jude 22

Pray about it: *Stop and ask God for a divine filling of his love. Ask for the perspective to see your ministry and the children in your community through eyes filled with love. Think about where can you take your ministry out of the four walls of the church and into the community to show God's love in a tangible way.*

_____

_____

_____

_____

_____

_____

WHAT A YEAR!
KEEP MAKING A DIFFERENCE

And let's consider how to
ENCOURAGE
one another in love and good deeds, not
abandoning our own meeting together,
as is the habit of some people, but
encouraging **ONE ANOTHER**; and all the
more as you see the day drawing near.
-Hebrews 10:24-25

Pray about it: How have you seen God move in the past year?

_____

_____

_____

_____

_____

_____

_____

_____

_____

_____

_____

CPSIA information can be obtained
at www.ICGtesting.com
Printed in the USA
BVHW040837221221
624590BV00016BA/653